If
you want
to evaluate
your
library . . .

by

F. W. Lancaster
University of Illinois

1988
University of Illinois
Graduate School of Library and Information Science
249 Armory Building
505 E. Armory Street
Champaign, IL 61820-6291

Printed in the United States of America

Distributed exclusively by
University of Illinois
Graduate School of Library and Information Science
249 Armory Building
505 E. Armory Street
Champaign IL 61820-6291
USA

Library of Congress Catalog Card Number 88-091-099

ISBN 0-87845-078-5

To my family

If
you want
to evaluate
your
library . . .

Contents

List of Exhibits

Preface

In 1977 my book *The Measurement and Evaluation of Library Services* was published by Information Resources Press. Happily, it earned favorable reviews, was adopted as a text by several schools of library and information science, and received the American Library Association's Ralph Shaw Award as an outstanding contribution to the literature of library science.

Despite all this, I have never felt the book to be completely satisfactory for use as a text in a course on this subject. It is a review and synthesis of earlier literature rather than a practical guide to the conduct of evaluations within libraries.

The present book has evolved from almost twenty years of experience in teaching courses at the University of Illinois and elsewhere. It is intended primarily as a text to support such courses, and includes study questions for the use of students. Nevertheless, I hope it will also be of value to librarians interested in performing studies in their own libraries.

While I include many references to studies that I consider particularly important, or that serve to illustrate some point I wish to make, this book does not claim to be a comprehensive review of the literature. It should thus be regarded as a complement to *The Measurement and Evaluation of Library Services* rather than a replacement for it.

As usual, I need to express my deep gratitude to Kathy Painter for her fine work in the typing of this text.

F.W. Lancaster
Urbana, Illinois
January 1988

The Author

F. Wilfrid Lancaster has been a professor in the Graduate School of Library and Information Science, University of Illinois, since 1970.

He is the author of eight previous books on various facets of library and information science, several of which have been translated into Russian, Chinese, Japanese, Arabic, and Spanish. Three of them received the Best Information Science Book award of the American Society for Information Science. An earlier book on the evaluation of library services received the American Library Association's Ralph R. Shaw Award as an outstanding contribution to the literature of library science.

Professor Lancaster received the Outstanding Information Science Teacher award from the American Society for Information Science in 1980, the first year the award was made.

1. Introduction

A typical dictionary may define *evaluation* as "assessing the value" of some activity or object. Authors dealing with the subject of evaluation, however, are likely to be more precise. Some claim that evaluation is a branch of research—the application of "the scientific method" to determine, for example, how well a program performs. Others stress its role in decision-making: the evaluation gathers data needed to determine which of several alternative strategies appears most likely to achieve a desired result. Finally, some writers look upon evaluation as an essential component of management; in particular, the results of an evaluation may help the manager to allocate resources more effectively.

These various viewpoints, of course, are quite compatible. Moreover, they all tend to emphasize the *practical* nature of evaluation. An evaluation is performed not as an intellectual exercise but to gather data *useful* in problem-solving or decision-making activities.

A good way to focus on the evaluation of library services is through a generalized representation of the operations of a library as seen through the eyes of an evaluator (Exhibit 1). The long-term objective of the library,* presumably, is to produce certain *outcomes* in the community to be served. While certain desired *outcomes* will be the raison d'être for its existence, the library is more directly concerned with the processing of *inputs* in order to generate *outputs*, which are the information services it provides. The primary input, financial resources, is used to acquire major secondary inputs, namely information resources* (mostly publications of various types), personnel to exploit these resources, and physical facilities to store materials, offer services, and so on.

The operation of the library can be considered as essentially a marriage between the information resources and the personnel: the system consists primarily of information resources and of people skilled in the exploitation of these resources on behalf of the users. Two

---

*Much of what is discussed in this book as applying to libraries could also apply to other kinds of information services. The term "library," then, is used as a shorthand for "libraries and other information centers." Similarly, "information resources" is used as a generic term to represent sources of information, inspiration, and recreation.
Note that a slightly different version of this chapter is to appear in the book *The Theory and Practice of Information Science*, edited by J. Olsgaard, to be published by the American Library Association in 1988.

principal groups of activities are identified in the diagram as taking
place within the library. The first is concerned with organization and
control of information resources. These activities—usually referred to
as "technical services" in a traditional library setting—produce various
tools (catalogs, bibliographies, shelf classification, and the like) that
make possible the second group of activities, the public services.

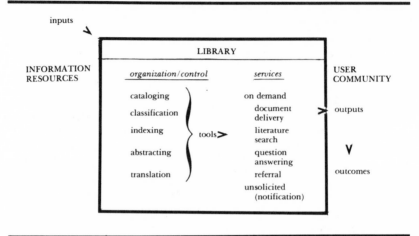

Exhibit 1
The operations of a library

The public services have been divided into two groups: "on
demand" services and "notification" services. The former can be considered passive services in the sense that they respond to demands rather
than initiate them. The notification services, on the other hand, are
more dynamic; they are designed to inform people of publications and
other information sources likely to be of interest to them. The on
demand services themselves fall into two major groups: document delivery and information retrieval services. The notification services are
primarily retrieval services or, more correctly, information dissemination services.

The library, then, can be looked upon as an interface between the
available information resources and the community of users to be
served. Therefore, any evaluation applied to the library should be
concerned with determining to what extent it successfully fulfills this
interface role.

Inputs, Outputs, and Outcomes

For evaluation purposes, a library can be studied in a number of different ways. Exhibit 1 implies that an evaluation program might look at inputs, at outputs, or at outcomes. The sequence *input, output, outcome* is one of increasing complexity. One would usually like to determine to what extent the desired outcomes of a service have been attained. Unfortunately, the desired outcomes will tend to relate to long-term social, behavioral, or even economic objectives that are rather intangible and, therefore, not easily converted into concrete evaluation criteria. For example, a desired outcome in one institution might be "to improve the quality of teaching and research within the institution" while another might seek to "keep researchers and practitioners abreast with the latest developments in their fields of specialization." Regrettably, while long-term objectives of this kind should provide the justification for the existence of information services, it is virtually impossible to measure the degree to which they are achieved. Even if the measurements were possible, one could not readily isolate the contribution made by the service itself. In short, one would do well to abandon the idea of using desired outcomes as *direct* criteria for the evaluation of libraries and other information services. Drucker (1973), in fact, has suggested that this situation will apply in the evaluation of any public service institution.

In contrast to outcomes, the inputs are tangible and easily quantified. Indeed, both primary and secondary inputs are inherently quantitative rather than qualitative in nature. That is, the inputs have little value in and of themselves—they can only be evaluated in terms of the role that they play in achieving desired outputs.

The most obvious example of this, perhaps, is the collection of books and other materials that can be considered the major input to a library. Such collections cannot be evaluated in the abstract but only in relation to the purposes they are intended to serve and the actual needs existing in the population of potential users. In other words, the collection (input) must be evaluated in terms of the extent to which it satisfies the demands placed upon it (i.e., output); any other evaluation criteria would be artificial and meaningless.

The outputs of the library—i.e., the services provided—are less tangible than the inputs but much more tangible than the outcomes. The outputs are easily quantified—e.g., number of documents delivered, number of referrals made, number of literature searches performed, number of questions answered—but this is not enough. Unlike inputs, the outputs can and must be evaluated in terms of quality. Thus, for each service provided, qualitative criteria of success should be identified.

This brings us back to the outcomes of an information service. While these cannot be studied directly, the criteria used to evaluate outputs should be good *predictors* of the extent to which the desired outcomes are achieved. Take, for example, a current awareness service, such as a Selective Dissemination of Information (SDI) system. The desired outcome is to make users better informed and more up-to-date in their area of specialization. The achievement of this objective is not easily measured directly. However, the desired outcome strongly suggests what the evaluation criteria should be at the output level. It seems reasonable to assume that the more items the service brings to the attention of users that are directly related to their interests (and, conversely, the fewer that are not directly related), the more likely it is that the users will become better informed. Further, the more of these items that are new to the user (i.e., items of which he was previously unaware), the more likely it is that the service is succeeding in keeping the user up-to-date. Thus, two evaluation criteria for this output (service)— *relevance* (or pertinence) and *novelty*—have been identified that seem also to be good predictors of the extent to which the desired outcome is reached.

Clearly, the interrelationship that exists among inputs, outputs, and outcomes has important implications for the design of information systems and services. One should begin by defining what it is that the system is intended to achieve. These are the desired outcomes. One then determines what services (outputs) are needed to produce these outcomes, and how these services can be provided most efficiently and economically. This leads to the identification of the inputs necessary to achieve the desired outputs. The criteria used to evaluate these services should predict the extent of attainment of the outcomes that guided their establishment. For document delivery services, presumably, the output measure would be the number of document needs satisfied (i.e., the extent to which the service can supply publications to users at the time they are needed); for question-answering services, it would be the percentage of questions answered completely and correctly; for referral services, it would be the percentage of referrals that leads users to appropriate sources of informaiton. Literature searches would be evaluated in terms of the relevance of the results to the information needs of the users and, for certain types of needs, the completeness of the results. It should be noted that some information services can be evaluated on a binary scale—either the user gets what he wants or he does not—while others can only be evaluated according to some form of graduated scale—for example, the proportion of items retrieved in a literature search that is directly relevant to the needs of the requester.

Just as qualitative measures of output can predict achievement of outcomes, certain input measures might be considered good predictors of desired outputs. For example, the more items that exist within the collections of the library, the more document delivery needs are likely to be satisfied; the larger the collection of reference tools, the more questions that could be answered completely and correctly, and so on.

Indeed, it is possible to use certain evaluation methods, applied to input, that are intended to simulate an output situation and thus approximate an evaluation of output. For example, in evaluating the coverage of some portion of a collection against an external standard, such as an authoritative bibliography, one is in effect estimating the ability of the library to satisfy information needs of actual users in this subject. This is a legitimate approach *if* one can be sure that the external standard fully reflects the needs of the users of this particular collection.

Costs, Effectiveness, and Benefits

A somewhat different way of looking at evaluation is in terms of costs, effectiveness, and benefits. Effectiveness relates to outputs, and the overall criterion of effectiveness is the proportion of user demands that are satisfied. The benefits of the system are really the desired outcomes. Costs are quite tangible as long as one thinks only in monetary terms. But it is easy to be myopic in this respect. One should avoid the fallacy that time spent *using* information services is free. User time is not free, at least not within the broad context of society as a whole. In point of fact, the cost of operating an information service may be quite small compared with the cost of *using* it.* For certain evaluation purposes, a realistic cost analysis of an information service should take all costs—including those incurred by users—into account. This point will be pursued further later in the chapter.

At a national level, costs incurred by all components of the system may need to be considered. Suppose, for example, that a library, *A*, requests photocopies from a particular periodical from other libraries ten times a year. From *A*'s point of view, it may be cheaper to do this than to subscribe to that periodical. However, from the viewpoint of the national system as a whole—taking the costs of all components into account—it may be cheaper for *A* to pay the subscription and handling costs.

Cost can be related to effectiveness or to benefits. *Cost-effectiveness* refers to the costs of achieving a particular level of effectiveness within

---

*See Braunstein (1979) as one example of the discussion of user costs.

an information service. Some type of unit cost measure will be needed. Examples of cost-effectiveness measures would include cost per document delivered to users, cost per question answered successfully, cost per relevant item retrieved in a literature search, and so on. The cost-effectiveness of a service can be improved by holding costs constant while raising the level of effectiveness or by maintaining a particular level of effectiveness while reducing the costs.

Cost-effectiveness, then, relates to optimization in the allocation of resources—the better the allocation of resources, the better the quality of service (i.e., effectiveness) that is achieved for a particular level of expenditure. In this connection, one must recognize that it is unrealistic to expect an information system to satisfy every need of every user. The concept of the "90% library" is an important one (Bourne, 1965). That is, one can design a service that will satisfy some reasonable percentage of all demands—perhaps as much as 90%—but to go beyond that would require a completely disproportionate level of expenditure. For example, 200 periodical titles may satisfy 90% of the needs for periodical articles in a particular institution, but 500 may be needed to satisfy 95% of the needs, and 1200 to satisfy 99%. The "90% library" is discussed further in Chapter 13.

A cost-benefit evaluation relates the benefits (outcomes) of a service to the cost of providing it. Again, the cost-benefit relationship can be improved by increasing benefits without increasing costs or by reducing costs without reducing benefits. In the long-term, however, a cost-benefit study attempts to demonstrate that the benefits derived from a service outweigh the costs of providing it. Because, as suggested earlier, the benefits of information services tend to be intangible, and not easily expressed in the same unit as the costs (e.g., $), true cost-benefit studies are virtually unattainable in our field. Nevertheless, attempts have been made with varying degrees of success. Cost-effectiveness and cost-benefit analysis are dealt with in Chapters 13 and 14.

While most managers would like to be able to prove that the services they provide can be justified from a cost-benefit point of view, the difficulties involved in such a study have discouraged all but a few attempts of this kind. For this reason, this book will focus on outputs and effectiveness rather than outcomes or benefits.

Purpose of Evaluation

There exist a number of possible reasons why the managers of a library may wish to conduct an evaluation of the services provided. One is simply to establish a type of "benchmark" to show at what level of performance the service is now operating. If changes are subsequently made to the services, the effects can then be measured against the benchmark previously established. A second, and probably less common, reason is to compare the performance of several libraries or services. Since a valid comparison of this type implies the use of an identical evaluation standard, the number of possible applications of this kind of study tends to be quite limited. Examples include comparison of the coverage of different data bases, the comparative evaluation of the document delivery capabilities of several libraries, and the use of a standard set of questions to compare the performance of question-answering services. A third reason for evaluation of an information service is simply to justify its existence. A justification study is really an analysis of the benefits of the service or an analysis of the relationship between the benefits and the cost. The fourth reason for evaluation is to identify possible sources of failure or inefficiency in the service with a view to raising the level of performance at some future date. Using an analogy with the field of medicine, this type of evaluation can be regarded as diagnostic and therapeutic. In some ways it is the most important type. Evaluation of an information service is a sterile exercise unless conducted with the specific objective of identifying means of improving its performance.

Evaluation Methods

An evaluation of an information service may be subjective or objective. Subjective studies—based on opinions—are not without value because it is important to know how people feel about a service. But an evaluation is of most value if it is analytical and diagnostic, seeking to discover how the service might be improved, and it is difficult to base this type of study on opinion alone. In general, then, objective criteria and procedures should be followed. The results of an objective study should be quantifiable.

Evaluation studies can involve real users in real institutional settings. Alternatively, various simulations are possible. If "real" studies are employed, the evaluator can try to get all users to participate on a voluntary basis or can use random sampling to focus on a set of representative users. The latter is much to be preferred. It is better to get reliable data from a few users than to gather less reliable data from many.

For certain evaluation purposes, too, it may be sufficient that evaluation data be anonymous while, for other purposes, this may not be good enough. For example, materials left on tables in a library may reflect materials consulted in that library but tell us nothing about who used them and for what purpose. Randomized interviews with people using materials within a library give qualitatively different data that may be essential in answering certain types of questions concerning in-house use of the collection.

If carefully designed, simulation studies can provide much valuable information without disturbing the users of the system at all. A good example is the "document delivery test" (Orr et al., 1968a). A list of bibliographic references, say 300, forms the basis of a search in a particular library on a particular day. The search determines how many items are owned and how many of the items owned are actually available on the shelves. In effect, the test simulates 300 users walking into the library that day, each one looking for a single item. As long as the 300 references are fully representative of the needs of the users of that library (not too difficult to achieve in the case of a special library, much more difficult for a general library), the simulation can give excellent data on the probability of ownership and the probability of availability. Other simulations can be devised for other information services, including question-answering and literature searching.

The Five Laws of Library Science

Elsewhere (Lancaster and Mehrotra, 1982), I have described how Ranganathan's Five Laws of Library Science (Ranganathan, 1931) can guide decisions on what should be evaluated, by what criteria, and by what methods. These laws provide a fundamental statement of the goals that information services should strive for, and they are as relevant today as they were fifty years ago.

The first law, Books Are For Use, seems obvious but it is a law to which libraries don't always adhere. Ranganathan, himself, deplored the fact that many librarians seemed to be more concerned with preservation than with use, thus perpetuating the image of the librarian as a custodian rather than as someone skilled in the exploitation of bibliographic resources. The most obvious implication of the law is that one must evaluate collections and services in terms of the needs of users. Moreover, it suggests that objective, empirical investigation should replace purely subjective or impressionistic approaches.

Carried to its logical conclusion, Books Are For Use implies considerations of cost-effectiveness. Because of limited resources, $30 spent on a book that is little if ever used is $30 less available for an item (possibly a duplicate copy) of something that might be in great demand. In the operation of information services, expected "cost per use" must be of paramount concern in deciding which items to add to a collection and which not to add. This situation is changing, however, as more and more bibliographic resources become accessible through electronic networks. The obvious implication of this, of course, is that "ownership," per se, is becoming less important in the evaluation of the resources of an information service. The evaluation criterion is "accessibility": can the service make an item accessible to a requester, at the time he or she needs it, from whatever source, in whatever acceptable form?

Ranganathan's second law, Every Reader His Book, is a logical extension of the first. Data on books borrowed or used in a library have an obvious limitation: they reflect only successes and tell us nothing about failures. That is, a book used represents, in some sense, a success. But volume of use is relatively meaningless unless one can convert it into a "satisfaction rate." To do this one must determine the probability that a user, looking for a particular item, or materials on a certain subject, will find this item or these materials available at the time needed. In other words, for everything looked for, how much is found (success) and how much is not found (failure)? The second law goes beyond collection evaluation and into the assessment of *availability*. It is not enough that an item sought by a user is owned by the library; it must also be available when needed.

Every Reader His Book can be considered a generic label that really means "Every reader his need." It can be extended to other types of needs of library users—e.g., what is the probability of having a factual question answered completely and correctly? This, too, can be handled by a simulation procedure in which the evaluator tests the library through a set of questions for which answers are already known (e.g., Crowley and Childers, 1971). In this case, the reference questions may be put to the library by volunteers posing as real users. The library is evaluated in terms of the number of questions answered completely and correctly.

The third law, Every Book Its Reader, complements the second. In relation to the second law, the library's role is relatively passive. Assuming that a user makes a demand on the library's services, the evaluator is concerned with whether or not the demand is satisfied. But libraries need to be more dynamic institutions. An important function should be that of making people aware of new publications of possible interest to them. Libraries should be concerned with *exposure* as well as with *accessibility* (Hamburg, 1974).

The significance of the third law is that books need to find their potential users as well as users the books they need. One could say that, for every item acquired by the library (and even, to carry this to its logical conclusion, for every item published), there are potential readers existing in the community. A library should therefore be evaluated in terms of its ability to inform people of the materials of potential use to them.

This is not such an easy evaluation exercise and, as a consequence, it is one rarely attempted. One obvious facet is simply the extent to which the library is able to achieve penetration in the community served—the extent to which its services are known, for example. More specifically, however, evaluation should be concerned with how successful the library is in informing users of newly acquired materials. If it produces a "new book list," how widely is it disseminated? Does it produce "targeted" bibliographies (e.g., new books on gardening) and, if so, do these reach the audiences who will most benefit (in this case, perhaps, gardening clubs)?

In special libraries and information centers a more personalized level of current awareness may exist, perhaps achieved through the use of computers to match the profile of a user's interests against characteristics of newly published literature (i.e., Selective Dissemination of Information). In this case, the evaluation criteria would be:

1) How much of what is brought to a user's attention is actually relevant to his interests?
2) How much of what is relevant was previously unknown to the user?
3) What proportion of the items brought to his attention does the user ask to see?

The fourth law, Save the Time of the Reader, virtually pervades all the others. Information services must be concerned not only with satisfying needs but with satisfying needs as efficiently as possible. It is now well known that the accessibility of information services is the major determinant of their use. Someone is likely to judge a service to be "inaccessible" if it requires too much effort to use (Mooers, 1960; Allen and Gerstberger, 1966, 1968).

A defect of many evaluations of library and information services is that they look upon user time as "free." This erroneous assumption completely invalidates certain cost-effectiveness analyses that have been performed. The time of users cannot be considered free since the time they spend using library materials could be spent in other, and, in some cases, more productive ways. In their analyses of the scientific and technical communication system in the United States, King et al. (1976) showed that the cost of *using* (i.e., reading) publications greatly exceeds the cost of producing and distributing them. By the same token, the cost of *using* the library greatly exceeds the cost of the collection, staff, and physical facilities. This can be seen most clearly in the case of a library within industry or government. If a scientist or engineer visits the library to use materials for, say, one hour, it may cost the library $5 in staff time (to assist the user) and other resources expended, but it actually may cost the organization $50, when the user's time (including all overheads) is figured into the calculations.

In the evaluation of library services, the time of the user must be given sufficient weight. Moreover, in the cost-effectiveness analysis of information services, all costs, including all user costs, must usually be taken into account. To do otherwise could lead to completely erroneous conclusions. For certain types of evaluation, in fact, an information service cannot be treated in isolation but must be looked at within the context of the larger community of which it forms a part. This is particularly important in any cost-effectiveness or cost-benefit analyses.

The fifth and final law, The Library is a Growing Organism, indicates that the library must be willing to adapt to new conditions. This would include adaptability to changing social conditions and technological developments. For the evaluator, this implies examining how long the library takes to adopt innovation, including adoption of new publication forms and new forms of information distribution. Modern computer and telecommunications technologies are changing our very concept of "library." Indeed, as mentioned earlier, providing some form of online access to materials on demand seems gradually to be replacing access through "ownership." That is, *access* rather than *ownership* should be the main criterion by which a library's "resources" should be evaluated.

Libraries should also be evaluated in terms of the extent to which they are able to capitalize on the capabilities provided by technology. For example, one important advantage of automated systems is that, if properly designed, they can provide many data to aid decision-making and generally to improve the management process. Another facet is the ability of a library to exploit technology in order to provide services that it had not been able to offer earlier (e.g., a high level of literature searching support made possible by online access to a wide range of data bases).

There is another aspect to adaptation that must be considered, namely the ability of the library to adapt to changing needs among its clientele. In this connection there is a danger that must be recognized and guarded against. Library services cannot be evaluated solely in relation to the demands placed upon them by present users. Such evaluation accepts demands at face value and assumes that these demands are co-extensive with user *needs*, which is not invariably true. Moreover, present users of a library may have needs for materials or information that, for one reason or another, are never converted into demands on the library's services. Finally, there are people who make no use of the library's services. If evaluation activities focus only on the demands (i.e., expressed needs) of present users and fail to study the needs lying behind these demands, or if they ignore the latent needs that are not converted into demands as well as the potential needs of present nonusers, the danger exists of creating a self-reinforcing situation. That is, the library is constantly improving its ability to respond to the present type of demand and, by so doing, perhaps reducing its ability to attract new users or new uses of the resources available. Such a library is far from being a growing organism.

The Need for Evaluation

Line (1979) has expressed the opinion that academic libraries (at least) do not observe Ranganathan's Five Laws. Indeed, he maintains that they tend to observe their own set of five laws, more or less diametrically opposed to Ranganathan's, namely:

1. Books are for collecting
2. Some readers their books
3. Some books their readers
4. Waste the time of the reader
5. The library is a growing mausoleum

While this may seem somewhat facetious, there is undoubtedly some truth in Line's claims. For many years libraries operated in an environment largely free from objective evaluation. If few serious complaints were received, one tended to assume that the service was satisfactory. Such an assumption was frequently erroneous but librarians, lacking objective performance measures and methods, became somewhat complacent about their services. When objective evaluation procedures were first applied to library and information services, some of the results shocked many people—e.g., the finding that a user may have less than a 50% chance that a sought item is immediately available in a library, or less than a 60% chance that his factual question will be answered completely and correctly.

The fact is that evaluation is an essential element in the successful management of any enterprise. Ranganathan's fifth law provides the major justification for evaluative activities. Healthy growth implies adaptation to changing conditions and adaptation implies evaluation to determine what changes need to be made and how they may best be accomplished. Electronic technology has already produced new forms of publications and new media for the distribution of publications and information. It is likely that the developments of the next two decades will be even more dramatic than those of the last two. The ability to distribute information rapidly and inexpensively in electronic form is threatening the entire raison d'être of the library. The library must be evaluated not only in terms of "how is it doing" but in terms of "is it doing what it should be doing?" That is, the library profession must look at its functions critically to determine if it is playing a role appropriate to the last quarter of the twentieth century or one more appropriate to the first quarter.

Evaluation is not an end in itself. An evaluation should only be performed with definite objectives in mind. This will usually mean that a study is designed to answer certain specific questions and to gather data to allow system improvements to be made. An evaluation can be expensive if it is diffuse and lacks well-defined objectives but need not be unreasonably expensive if it is sharply focused. Moreover, the investment made in a careful evaluative study can be fully justified if the results reveal what may need to be done to improve the effectiveness or cost-effectiveness of the service or its relevance to the present needs of the community.

Diagnostic Evaluation

From the evaluator's point of view, even the simplest of library services is really quite complicated in that many factors may influence whether or not the service is successful in meeting the needs of a particular user. Consider, for example, Exhibit 2, which shows a user entering a library in order to borrow a particular item—a book, periodical article, or whatever—for which there is no substitute. The evaluator would like to know whether or not the user leaves the library "happy" which, in this case, probably means having the item in hand. Here, it is the document delivery function of the library, or at least one aspect of it, that is being evaluated.

This "known item search" situation is outwardly rather simple. Nevertheless, it is not quite as simple as it appears at first sight. In fact, whether or not the user is successful depends upon the answers to a series of questions, the most important of which are explicitly represented in the diagram. Before the user can leave the library with the item, it must be owned by the library; the user must be able to find its shelf location, which will usually mean that the item has been cataloged and that the user can find an entry for it in the catalog (or a librarian can find such an entry for the user); the book must be available to the user—"on the shelf"; and he must be able to find it on the shelf.

Exhibit 2
The situation of a user entering a library to look
for a particular bibliographic item

A convenient way of looking at this situation is to consider it as a series of probabilities. What is the probability that the item will be owned, that it will be cataloged, that it will be found in the catalog, that it will be on the shelf, that it will be found on the shelf? Clearly, the probability that the user will leave the library "happy" is the product of these five component probabilities.

This can be illustrated by means of a simple example. Suppose that the library owns, on the average, 90% of the items sought by users (i.e., the "probability of ownership" is .9), that 80% of owned items can be located in the catalog, that 75% of these are on the shelf when users look for them, and that users succeed in finding items on the shelf (when actually present there) 90% of the time. The probability that a particular user will leave the library with an item sought is, thus, .9 x .8 x .75 x .9, or .486. That is, a user of this library faces about a 48% probability that he can find a particular item that he looks for.

One of the objectives of an evaluation is to establish probabilities of this kind. By performing a suitable study, one might determine that, of 500 bibliographic items looked for by users in a particular period of time, 450 were actually owned by the library. The success rate is therefore .9 (450/500), or 90%. Providing the sample used is truly representative of the diversity of document needs within the community, the study has established a probability of ownership of .9 for the library. In other words, a user entering the library to look for any particular item will face a probability of .9 that it will be owned. Similar studies can be performed in order to establish the other probabilities implicit in Exhibit 2: that the user can find an entry in the catalog, that an item will be available on the shelf when needed, and so on.

Unfortunately, strength in one aspect of the situation depicted in Exhibit 2 may cause problems elsewhere. The larger the size of the collection, for example, the greater the probability of ownership. But the larger the collection, the larger and more complicated will be the catalog, leading perhaps to a higher rate of failure in catalog use, at least for catalogs in card or printed form (the size factor may have a less dramatic effect in the case of an online catalog).

The questions raised in Exhibit 2 also reflect various facets of evaluation. "Is item owned?" implies an evaluation of the collection, the next two questions imply some form of catalog use study, and the last two questions refer to a study of "shelf availability." One can look at each part of the diagram separately (e.g., performing only a collection evaluation) or undertake a study to look at all parts at once (e.g., by interviewing a sample of users to establish success rate and to find where failures occur).

The probabilities mentioned earlier are based on averages for a significant number of events. A "probability of ownership of .9," for example, refers to a probability that applies to all users and uses of the library. A score of this kind, however, might vary considerably with such factors as type of user, type of document, age of material, and subject matter. In the academic environment, a particular library might satisfy 99% of undergraduate needs for publications but only 65% of doctoral student needs. The score is also likely to fluctuate with type of publication. For example, the probability of ownership might be 1.0 for U.S. patents, .9 for periodical articles, .78 for books, .32 for technical reports, and so on.

This brings us to a very important point. To be useful, an evaluative study must do more than indicate what the "score" of the library is for some service. It must also provide data that indicate how that score fluctuates when conditions change. Put somewhat differently, the study should demonstrate under what conditions the service performs well and under what conditions it performs badly, thereby allowing identification of the most efficient ways to improve performance. This type of evaluation can be considered diagnostic.

The most important element of diagnosis is the identification of reasons why particular failures occur. A user might not be able to find an entry in the catalog, even though it is actually present there, because cards have been misfiled, the user does not have complete or correct information, the catalog has inadequate cross-references, the user lacks familiarity with the catalog, or any of several other possible reasons. Similarly, a book sought may not be on the shelf because another user has already borrowed it, because it is waiting to be reshelved, because it is being re-bound, because it is missing, and so on.

If an evaluation is to be more than an academic exercise, it should be diagnostic, collecting data that indicate how a service performs and why it performs as it does, including reasons why failures occur. A diagnostic evaluation, then, should be of practical use to the librarian, providing guidance on what actions might be taken to improve the effectiveness of the services provided.

This book discusses methods that can be used to evaluate various facets of library service, both the determination of *success rate* (i.e., establishing the probabilities referred to earlier) and the identification of reasons for successes and failures (i.e., diagnosis). Those facets that relate primarily to "document delivery" (including the collection of a library and the catalog of that collection) are dealt with first, followed by reference services. The remaining chapters cover related evaluation topics, including cost-effectiveness and cost-benefit aspects.

Study Questions

1. For different types of library try to identify several desired outcomes for the services provided. What output measures might be reasonable predictors of the extent to which these outcomes are achieved?

2. Consider the library that you use most frequently. Do you have any evidence that this library observes Ranganathan's "five laws?" Do you have any evidence that Line's alternative laws are obeyed?

2. Evaluation of the Collection: Formulae, Expert Judgment, and Use of Bibliographies

The collection of materials held is the component of library service that has been most subject to evaluation over the years. One reason is the obvious importance of the collection to all library activities. A second is the fact that the collection is something concrete and this makes it appear simpler to evaluate than the services provided through exploitation of the collection, which seem inherently more "abstract."

Nevertheless, as suggested in Chapter 1, one cannot evaluate a collection in isolation but only in terms of its value to the users of the library. At least, this is true if one accepts the fact that books are "for use" rather than "for collecting."

Based on methods used in the past, one can classify the major approaches to collection evaluation as follows:

1. Quantitative
   Size
   Growth
2. Qualitative
   Expert judgment
   Bibliographies used as standards*
       Published bibliographies
       Specially-prepared bibliographies
   Analysis of actual use

Quantitative Considerations

One obvious criterion for the evaluation of a collection is its size. All other things being equal, one would expect that the larger the collection the greater the chance that it will contain a particular item sought by a user. This is especially true in the case of libraries designed to support research. Minimum standards for collection size in libraries of various types have been put forward by different organizations, including agencies of accreditation. Standards of this type tend to be related to the size of the population served by the library. Thus, "books

---

*Bibliographies can be used to evaluate a collection or to study the degree to which two or more collections overlap.

per capita" is a measure sometimes used, especially by public libraries. Such measures can be meaningful as long as the "books" referred to are likely to be of use or interest to the community served. However, a public library could achieve a high "books per capita" figure by buying large quantities of cheap books of low quality, by indiscriminately accepting many donations, or by never discarding books that are old and unused, none of which is likely to produce a collection of maximum value to the community.

In any case, "books per capita" is a very simplistic formula to use in calculating the minimum or optimum size for the collection of a public library. More sophisticated and elaborate procedures have been proposed by various authors, including McClellan (1978), Stoljarov (1973), and Betts and Hargrave (1982).

A recent study by Detweiler (1986) suggests that a collection of 100,000 volumes may be "optimum" for a public library when number of circulations per volume is the criterion. Between 50,000 and 100,000 volumes, a "dramatic increase in circulation per volume added" can be observed, but no such relationship is discernible in the range of 100,000 to 150,000. Above 150,000 volumes, there is some evidence of a negative correlation between collection size and circulation.

The situation is more complicated in academic libraries. It makes little sense in this setting to treat each user as equal, since faculty, doctoral students, and others engaged in research are likely to need a level of bibliographic support an order of magnitude greater than that required by undergraduates. Collection size here, then, needs to be related to the number, size, and complexity of the academic programs. This has led to the development of various formulae for calculating the minimum size of the collection in a particular academic library.

The first such formula to be widely used was devised by Clapp and Jordan (1965). As McInnis (1972) has shown, the formula can be written as a weighted sum of several variables:

$$V = 50{,}750 + 100F + 12E + 12H + 335U + 3{,}050M + 24{,}500D$$

where

- F = number of faculty
- E = total number of students enrolled
- H = number of undergraduate honors students
- U = number of major undergraduate subjects
- M = master's fields offered
- D = doctoral fields offered
- V = volumes

and 50,750 is a constant, representing a minimum viable university library in number of volumes.

Note that the Clapp-Jordan formula takes into account several factors affecting required size of collection and gives greatest weight to those likely to lead to the most stringent demands on the collection. Thus, number of doctoral fields exerts a profound influence—too much according to some critics (McInnis, 1972), especially when one considers that "doctoral field" is subject to different interpretations in different institutions.

Several variants or refinements of the Clapp-Jordan formula have been developed and used. The Association of College and Research Libraries (ACRL) has included a similar formula in its "Standards for College Libraries" (1986). It specifies a core collection of 85,000 volumes with additional increments determined as follows: 100 volumes per full time equivalent (FTE) faculty member, 15 volumes per FTE student, 350 volumes per undergraduate major or minor, 6,000 volumes per master's program where no higher degree is offered in this field, 3,000 volumes in a master's program in which a higher degree is also offered, 6,000 volumes for fields in which sixth year specialist degrees exist, and 25,000 volumes per doctoral field. Associated with this formula is a grading scheme for academic collections. A library is an *A* library if it owns at least 90% of the recommended number of volumes, a *B* library if it owns 75-89%, a *C* library if it owns 60-74%, and a *D* library if it owns 50-59%. The formula can be applied to different academic departments. Thus, a university may find itself an *A* library in, say, education but a *D* library in engineering (Burr, 1979).

Unfortunately, quantitative standards or formulae of this type can be subject to misinterpretation. Although they are intended to prescribe *minimum* requirements, some bodies responsible for funding have been known to use them against the library, reducing levels of financial support on the grounds that the library already exceeds the standards. So, some of the substandard libraries may benefit by using the formulae to show how much they need to improve, while some of the better libraries could actually suffer financially as a result of comparison with the standards.

Another problem associated with quantitative standards, of course, is the possible imprecision of the unit of measurement: "the volume." For example, should a 5-page pamphlet be given the same weight in the score as a 500-page monograph, how are microfiche to be counted, how are patents? The ACRL standards give minimum guidance on these problems.

One could also argue that the "title" is a more meaningful unit than the "volume" in comparing institutions, especially perhaps in the public library environment. Through purchase of multiple copies of bestsellers and other popular but probably ephemeral items, library *A* could have many more volumes than *B* but fewer titles. Library *B*, however, may have a superior collection in the sense of being richer, better balanced, and more able to meet the needs of a wide variety of users. However, a public library having several branches will need multiple copies of certain items in order to achieve a balanced collection in each location. In the academic world, some evidence exists that the larger the collection the greater the proportion of duplicates it is likely to have (Drone, 1984).

The size of a collection, in any case, means rather little unless current rate of growth is also considered. A long-established library, while very large, could perform poorly in meeting user needs because it is no longer spending enough on new acquisitions. Piternick (1963) argues that rate of growth should be considered in terms of number of volumes rather than percentage increase in the size of the collection. In fact, he presents data that suggest that academic excellence correlates positively with size of collection and with number of volumes added but not with percentage increase in collection size. One obvious reason is the fact that percentage rate of growth tends to be much greater for newer and smaller libraries than for the older, larger institutions (Baumol and Marcus, 1973). "Percentage rate of growth" is heavily affected by the weeding policies of various libraries. Voigt (1975) has presented a rather elaborate formula for calculating the rate at which university libraries should be acquiring new materials. A good review of the topic of growth of academic libraries is given by Molyneux (1986).

In the academic environment, a positive correlation has also been found between size of library and the quality of the institution, where "quality" is determined by some established scale of academic excellence (see, for example, Jordan, 1963; Blau and Margulies, 1974-75; and Piternick, 1963). This does not prove that the university or college is great because of its library, but the very fact that library size and academic excellence tend to "go together" gives some credibility to the claim that size is one criterion that has some applicability in the evaluation of collections.

Expert Judgment

One possible way of evaluating the holdings of a library in a particular subject area is to have the collection examined by a specialist in that field, a procedure sometimes referred to as "impressionistic."

The expert could be an outside consultant or a member of the institution itself; a team of specialists could replace the individual in a study of this type. The impressionistic approach has mostly been used in the evaluation of academic and other research libraries.

There are some obvious problems associated with this approach. A subject specialist may not be completely unbiased. Consequently, his evaluation may favor certain aspects or viewpoints within the field, while neglecting others. A subject specialist is not necessarily an expert on the *literature* of that subject, a situation that may be more true in some fields than in others. Moreover, as suggested earlier, the evaluation of a collection requires more than a knowledge of the literature; it requires a thorough understanding of the needs of the users of a particular library. The subject specialist may know the literature well but lack familiarity with the community the library is to serve. This seems especially likely where an outside consultant is used. Finally, if a university's own faculty members are involved in impressionistic evaluation, these may be the very individuals who were most responsible for building the collection in the first place; in this case, they would be evaluating their own efforts—a questionable practice at best.

One variant of the expert judgment approach involves the evaluation of a collection by members of the library staff, using formalized procedures to gather quantitative and qualitative data to assist in identifying areas of strength and weakness. For example, Mosher (1984) describes a method for the systematic analysis of collections, as used by a group of libraries in Alaska. For each class (e.g., economics) the following types of data are collected: number of items, variety of items (different document forms), age of materials, language, and, possibly, circulation records. At the same time, the team performing the analysis checks to see if, for example, "major" authors, works, and periodicals appear in the collection. Burr (1979) used similar methods in an analysis of the collections of an academic library. The data collected for each segment of the collection were: date of publication, language, type of publisher, and whether or not an item appears in a standard bibliography of recommended titles. Descriptive and quantitative data, if collected systematically in this way, can provide very useful input to any impressionistic study, whether conducted by librarians or outside consultants.

Bibliographies Used as Standards

In the impressionistic approach, the expert becomes a kind of "standard" used in the evaluation. In "list checking" or "citation checking," the standard used for evaluation is some type of bibliography, which is checked against the collection to determine what proportion of the items listed is owned.

The first problem faced, of course, is that of finding a suitable bibliography. A few "standard" lists have been compiled to meet special needs (e.g., of recommended books and journals for the small medical library). In other cases, authoritative bibliographies do exist (e.g., the *Cambridge Bibliography of English Literature* or the *Handbook of Latin American Studies*). Comer (1981) and Hall (1985) suggest a number of published bibliographies that may be applicable to various evaluation situations. An existing bibliographic source may be the clear choice for use in certain studies. Suppose one wanted to know how strong the medical libraries of Brazil are in their coverage of the journal literature of biomedicine. The obvious standard to use in answering this question is the National Library of Medicine's *List of Journals Indexed in Index Medicus*, which represents decisions made by a reputable and authoritative body on which journals are most worth indexing. However, even this list would need to be supplemented by a list of Brazil's own biomedical journals, since *Index Medicus* will not be comprehensive in its coverage of these. If the *List* was circulated to all important medical libraries in Brazil, and each indicated which journals they receive, one would discover:

a) what proportion of the journals on the list is accessible in Brazil,
b) how many copies of each title are to be found in Brazilian libraries,
c) which titles are not available in any of the medical libraries,
d) the comparative strengths of the various libraries in coverage of the periodical literature, and
e) the geographic distribution of the coverage (how strong the collections are in each region, each state, or each major city).

For many evaluation purposes, however, no published bibliography will exist. If one does exist, it may not be entirely suitable because it is not completely up-to-date, restricts itself to only one type of publication, has a somewhat different emphasis than that of the collation being evaluated, or for some other reason.

If no suitable published bibliography can be found, it will usually be possible to compile one specially for use in the study. Consider a situation in which one wants to know how strong is the collection of some academic library on the subject of Cuba—its history, international relations, culture, economics, and so on. One possible approach is to identify a number of scholarly books on various aspects of Cuba, recently published and reviewed favorably in reputable journals. Let us say that six such books are selected. The bibliographic items cited in them (in footnotes, chapter references, or final bibliography) can be assumed to represent the sources needed by the authors of these books in support of their research. Suppose that, once duplicates are eliminated, the six volumes yield 1350 bibliographic references. This list of 1350 items is checked against the collection to discover what proportion is owned. If 1110 of the 1350 items are found to be owned, the coverage of the collection on the subject of Cuba (more correctly, its coverage of information sources needed by Cuba scholars) has been estimated to be about 82%; put differently, the probability of ownership has been set at .82. Of course, the same bibliography of 1110 items could be used to compare the coverage of several libraries—to identify the strongest collections, the amount of duplication, and so on. The question one is attempting to answer in a study of this kind is really "could the research have been done in this library?" The "classic" study of this type is the work of Coale (1965) at the Newberry Library.

The method used by Coale is only really appropriate for the evaluation of collections intended to support research. However, Bland (1980) has pointed out that bibliographic references in college textbooks might be used in the evaluation of collections in small and medium sized academic libraries.

For some studies, especially in scientific and technical areas, journals are better than monographs as a source of bibliographic references because such references are likely to be more up-to-date.

Consider another problem: to evaluate the coverage of an academic medical library on the subject of "tropical medicine." A possible approach is as follows:

1. Identify those subject headings in *Index Medicus* that relate to tropical diseases and other aspects of tropical medicine.
2. Using the latest issues of *Index Medicus*, select a random sample of, say, 100 recently published journal articles appearing under the tropical medicine headings.
3. Acquire all of these articles, combine their bibliographies, and use this combined bibliogrpahy as the standard for evaluating the collection. If the mean number of references per article is 8, the bibliography is likely to exceed 700 items, even after elimination of duplicates, and this is large enough to give one confidence in the reliability of the results.*

The justification for this procedure is that the references appearing in recently indexed articles are likely to represent items that users will

---

*As an alternative to the *elimination* of duplicates, one might count the number of times a particular reference appears in the several bibliographies. The library evaluated would then get a coverage score, earning more "points" for having an item appearing on several of the bibliographies than it does for one appearing only in a single bibliography.

seek in a medical library. By looking for, say, 700 of these items, one is in effect simulating 700 users of the library, each one seeking a particular item.

In Step 2, as described above, it is important to obtain all items falling in the random sample, not just those readily available. For example, of the 100 items sampled, it may happen that only 75 are available in the library being evaluated. The other 25 should be obtained from other libraries. The reason is that a journal will tend to cite itself more than it cites other journals and more than other journals cite it. By drawing sources exclusively from journals owned by the library, the possibility exists that the sample will be biased in favor of the library. This was one defect of a study reported by Nisonger (1983), who drew references exclusively from six major political science journals likely to be in all political science collections of any size. This may not be too important in the comparison of libraries, since the standard remains the same for each, but it is likely to overestimate the completeness of any one collection.*

Because review articles usually contain more references than other types, it might be possible to restrict the sample to review articles. For example, in biomedicine, the sample could be drawn from the *Bibliography of Medical Reviews*..

The evaluation of a library collection in a specialized subject area is much the same as the evaluation of the coverage of a data base in machine-readable or printed form. Somewhat similar procedures could be used to evaluate the coverage of, say, *Biological Abstracts* in some specific subject. In fact, studies of this kind have been reported by Martyn (1967) and Martyn and Slater (1964).

Even if a "standard" bibliography on some subject exists, the specially-prepared bibliography has obvious advantages. This can be illustrated by another case: the coverage of an agriculture library on the subject of irrigation. An authoritative bibliography on irrigation would only cover the "core" of irrigation. But "literature of irrigation" is not quite the same as "literature needed to support research on irrigation," which is much broader in scope. By drawing samples of irrigation articles, and taking their references, one is assembling a bibliography that will include items dealing centrally with irrigation as well as items drawn from peripheral subject fields.

---

*In point of fact, this bias may not be as serious as one might think, as a recent study by Porta and Lancaster (1988) shows. Moreover, it is always possible to eliminate journal self-citations from the calculations.

The situation is illustrated in Exhibit 3. Writers on irrigation will cite sources on irrigation itself, on sciences closely related (agriculture, hydraulics), on other technical subjects, and on a wide variety of very peripheral topics (e.g., mathematics, statistics). The specially-prepared bibliography, then, provides a true test of the ability of the library to supply the wide range of materials needed to support research on irrigation. This is a more realistic evaluation than one focusing exclusively on the core of irrigation itself.

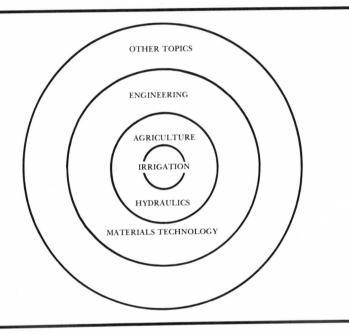

Exhibit 3
Sources cited in articles on irrigation

Many "standard" lists, besides concentrating solely on the core materials of some field, cover only those materials supposedly "the best" or "most obvious"—the kinds of things most libraries collecting in this area are likely to have. Such lists are of limited use as evaluative tools and of no use at all if they have been used by the library as tools in book selection.

It is not enough to use the list-checking approach solely to establish a probability of ownership. As emphasized in Chapter 1, evaluation should be diagnostic. In this case, the diagnostic element will involve a determination of what types of materials the library covers well and what types it does not cover well. That is, it will be necessary to compare the characteristics of the items owned with the characteristics of those not owned—by type of publication, by language, by date, by source, by subfield, by specificity—so that it will be possible to discover in what way the collection needs to be strengthened. It should be noted that diagnostic analysis of this kind requires larger samples than would be needed simply to establish a probability of ownership. A sample of 300 is quite reliable in estimating the coverage of a collection but one might need 1000 or more references to learn anything useful about what items or types of items are missing from the collection.

A more complex approach to the evaluation of an academic library collection has been used by Lopez (1983). It involves checking for ownership of a group of items, selecting references from those found, looking for these items, selecting more references, and so on, up to four or five levels of search. This method is illustrated in Exhibit 4.

Procedure	Number of references produced	Ideal score	Library owns	Possible score	Actual score
Select 5 books					
LEVEL 1 Select 20 references from each	100	5 x 100 = 500	80	500	5 x 80 = 400
LEVEL 2 Select *middle* reference from each of 80 found	80	10 x 100 = 1000	45	800	10 x 45 = 450
LEVEL 3 Select *first* reference from each of 45 found	45	20 x 100 = 2000	23	900	20 x 23 = 460
LEVEL 4 Select *last* reference from each of 23 found	23	40 x 100 = 4000	11	920	40 x 11 = 440
TOTALS	248	7500	159	3120	1750

Exhibit 4
The Lopez method of collection evaluation

The process begins with the selection of 5 books on some subject area. The books are chosen on the basis of their quality (as determined by reviews) and relevance to faculty research interests. From each, 20 references are selected from "different and staggered sections of the bibliographies" (Lopez is vague about how this is actually done). The 100 items thus identified are checked against the collection. In the hypothetical situation illustrated in Exhibit 4, 80 are found. The *middle** reference in each of the 80 is then located. Of these 80 references, the library is found to own 45. The *first* reference in each of these is selected, and so on up to four or five levels.

Note that the "ideal score" is the one that a library would achieve if it owned every item at each level. The "possible score," on the other hand, is the maximum score a library could achieve at each level after elimination of items not found at the preceding level. The scoring system depicted in Exhibit 4 represents a doubling of values from one level to the next. This is justified on the grounds that, as one moves from level to level, the material becomes older and more difficult to trace. This method of scoring might be considered appropriate for use in the humanities and social sciences. In science and technology, however, one would reverse the procedure, giving the higher scores to the earlier levels (more recent materials).

As Lopez applied the method, "library owns" implies more than location in the catalog. It means that the item was physically located, if necessary after repeated searches over several weeks.

The method is intriguing. However, the end result is merely a numerical score for the library (Lopez refers to it as a "qualitative index") that can then be compared with the "ideal" or "possible" scores. A numerical score of this kind would only have value in comparing two different libraries, using the same 5 books as the starting point in each, or comparing the collections of one library in different subject fields (i.e., with the starting point varied by use of books selected from different disciplines). Its value as a tool for comparison is diminished, however, if the method fails to give consistent results when different samples are drawn using the same procedures. Nisonger (1980) has found evidence that significantly different scores can be obtained when different references are selected from the books originally chosen. Nisonger, however, used smaller samples than those recommended by Lopez.

Other criticisms can be leveled at the technique. The selection of references at each level would be better achieved by random sampling.

---

*If all bibliographic references—in footnotes, at ends of chapters, etc.—were in one list, the one selected would be the one in the middle of the list.

More importantly, a possible bias exists in favor of the library being studied. The procedure would be much better if the evaluator obtained *every item at each level*, where necessary from other libraries, and drew a random sample from the complete universe of references at each level. As mentioned earlier, the tendency for self-citation (an author tends to cite himself, a journal tends to cite itself) may cause a bias if each succeeding level of references is chosen only from items known to be in the library. In fairness, however, it has not yet been proven that these changes would make any significant difference to the library score.

Some investigators have evaluated the collection of a university library on the basis of references contained in faculty publications or in doctoral dissertations produced in the university (e.g., Buzzard and New, 1983). This approach is of doubtful validity. Several investigations have shown that the "principle of least effort" has a major effect on information-seeking behavior: the more accessible an information source, the more likely it is to be used (Allen and Gerstberger, 1968; Rosenberg, 1966, 1967). More specifically, Soper (1972, 1976) has produced results to suggest that accessibility influences citation behavior— the more accessible the source, the more likely it is to be cited. If writers are more likely to cite sources readily available in their institutional library than to cite sources not so available, an evaluation of the collection on the basis of these citations introduces a definite bias in favor of the library. Rather than use internally generated dissertations, for example, it would be preferable to draw bibliographic references from those produced in comparable departments in other universities (i.e., departments with similar research interests). In terms of overall coverage, the difference between using internally produced dissertations and ones externally produced will not necessarily be dramatic (e.g., Popovich, 1978, estimated coverage at 88% based on the former and 84% based on the latter). Nevertheless, one is less likely to discover serious gaps in the collection, such as an important series of technical reports, from internal citation than one is from external.

Peat (1981) criticizes the procedures most frequently applied to measure in-house use of a library (see Chapter 4). He proposes that the bibliographic references appearing in faculty publications be taken as an indicator of which items added to a library's collection have received "research" use and which have not. This proposal assumes that all bibliographic items are equally "citable" and that items cited are the only ones used. The method Peat advocated has been used by McCain and Bobick (1981) in the evaluation of periodicals in a biology library.

The use of specially-prepared bibliographies is appropriate in evaluating the collection of a scholarly library on a subject by subject basis. It has little relevance, however, to public libraries because citation is not really applicable to much of the material that public libraries deal with. For instance, cookbooks tend not to cite other cookbooks, so it would be quite difficult to compile a bibliography useful in evaluating a library's collection of this type of publication. In point of fact, the specialized or scholarly library is easier to evaluate than the popular library: user needs tend to be more sharply defined, as well as more homogeneous, and it is easier to identify appropriate standards for evaluation (e.g., scholarly bibliographies). The public library presents much more complex problems because of its generality, the heterogeneity of the user community and the demands placed upon it by that community, and the lack of clear evaluation standards.

Nevertheless, Goldhor (1973, 1981b) has developed a different form of list checking that does have applicability in the public library environment. He points out that the titles checked against a list in some subject area may represent only a small percentage of a library's holdings in this field but the checking process tells us nothing about the other items in the collection. In Goldhor's "inductive method," rather than checking a list against the collection, portions of the collection are checked against reputable book-reviewing and other selection tools. The underlying assumption is that the more of these tools a book appears in, the more desirable it is, at least if the reviews are positive. It is thus possible to give each book checked a numerical score based upon the number of sources in which it appears. This procedure gives results quite different from those obtained through the bibliographic checking procedures discussed earlier. It may give some indication of the quality of a collection, but does not evaluate its coverage or suggest how the collection might be improved. It cannot be used to establish a probability of ownership—i.e., it tells us nothing about things that should perhaps be in the collection but are not. The inductive method is more applicable to the evaluation of "popular" collections (public libraries and perhaps undergraduate libraries) than it is to collections designed to support research, although a similar procedure was used by Burr (1979) as one element in the evaluation of the collections of a university library.

A new opportunity for collection evaluation arises from the widespread adoption of online bibliographic searching by libraries. Since the searches performed reflect current information needs of certain users, the bibliographic references retrieved can be considered to represent the current document needs of these users (i.e., if a search has been successful, the items retrieved will be those the requester will seek in the library). A library could use sampling of search results (selection of searches by random sampling, selection of references by random sampling, or both) as a means for the continuous monitoring of the collection. While this might be most applicable to a special library, it could also be useful in more general libraries, including public libraries. This measure was proposed, but not elaborated on, by Cronin (1985). One example of the use of this technique can be found in an article by Seba and Forrest (1978) who compared the results of online searches with library holdings to identify periodical titles held that appeared to be nonproductive as well as productive titles not held by the library. Sprules (1983), however, has discussed some of the problems involved in trying to use online searches to assist periodical cancellation decisions in an academic library. In a much earlier study Bourne and Robinson (1973) used printouts from a Selective Dissemination of Information (SDI) service in collection evaluation.

Various possible sources from which samples can be drawn for collection evaluation purposes have been reviewed in this chapter. A summary of the possibilities is given in Exhibit 5.

Bibliographies
 against collection

Standard lists

Specially prepared lists drawn from:

Monographs (Coale, Lopez)
College textbooks
Indexing/abstracting services
Selected journals (Nisonger)
Faculty/student publications
Results of bibliographic searches

Collections of other libraries
(overlap)

Collection
 against bibliographies

Inductive method
(Goldhor)

Exhibit 5
Sources for bibliographic checking

Overlap Studies

Studies of the degree to which the collection of one library overlaps those of others (i.e., of the extent of duplication of titles among libraries) have been performed for various purposes, as discussed by Potter (1982). Most overlap studies are not performed for collection evaluation per se, although they could be. Overlap studies applied to indexing and abstracting services, in printed or online form, have been undertaken in evaluating the coverage of these services (see, for example, Bourne, 1969; and Longo and Machado, 1981).

Suppose one wanted to compare the coverage of two abstracting services, both dealing with the subject of mental health. One can estimate the coverage of service *A* by drawing a random sample of items from service *B* and one can evaluate the coverage of service *B* on the basis of a random sample of items from *A*, as shown below:

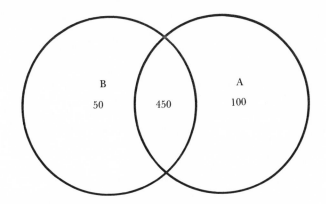

A random sample of 300, drawn from *A*, is checked against *B* and a random sample of 300, drawn from *B*, is checked against *A*. On the basis of these samples, the following hypothetical estimates are derived: that 450/600 (75%) are common to both, that 50/600 (8.3%) items are unique to *B*, and that 100/600 (16.6%) are unique to *A*. Another way of looking at this is to consider *A* as a standard for estimating the coverage of *B* and vice versa: using 300 items from *A* as a standard, *B*'s coverage of the mental health literature is estimated to be 66% (200/300); using 300 items from *B* as a standard, *A*'s coverage of this literature is estimated to be 83% (250/300).

In principle, there is no reason why a similar technique could not be used to estimate the coverage of the collection of a library, in some subject field. For example, the collection of gardening books in public library *A* could be evaluated on the basis of a random sample of gardening books from public library *B*. In this case, *B* could be considerably larger library than *A*. The objective is to determine how complete is collection *A* on the subject of gardening and to identify types of materials, or even specific titles, that *A* should have in its collection but does not.

Overlap studies can be used to compare the collections of libraries of all types and even to compare the coverage of libraries of different types. For example, for each of four Illinois communitites, Doll (1980) studied overlap and duplication among the public library collections and those of two elementary schools.

Sampling techniques for overlap studies become more complicated when many data bases or library collections are involved, or when the entire collection of one library is compared with the entire collection of another. These sampling problems are discussed in detail by Buckland et al. (1975).

In evaluating a collection by checking it against bibliographies, or against some other collection, one is treating it virtually in the abstract since *use* of the collection is not considered. Evaluation through use studies is dealt with in Chapters 3-6.

Study Questions

1. The College of Agriculture at the University of Illinois finds itself increasingly involved in supplying consultants to the less developed countries. Since many of the LDC's are situated in the tropics, demand for bibliographic support in the area of tropical agriculture is increasing. There is some feeling, however, that the coverage of the collection in this subject leaves much to be desired. You are asked to evaluate the collection in terms of its ability to support research/consulting in tropical agriculture, and to recommend how the collection in this area might be improved. What exactly would you do?

2. What procedures would you use to compare the coverage of tropical agriculture in two online data bases: **AGRICOLA** and **CAB** Abstracts?

3. A public library serving a population of about 100,000 is reputed to have an excellent collection of books on gardening. How might you confirm that this is true?

4. How would you compare a collection of science books held in the children's department of a public library with the science books held in the libraries of the local primary schools?

5. Would it be possible to derive a formula for the minimum size of a public library similar to the formulae developed for the size of academic libraries? What would be the components of such a formula?

3. Evaluation of the Collection: Analysis of Use

The approaches to evaluation discussed in Chapter 2 involve the comparison of a collection with some form of external standard. In the case of the bibliographic checking procedures, the study in effect simulates demands upon the library.

A completely different approach involves an analysis of how the collection is actually used. One objective is to identify strengths and weaknesses in the collection from present patterns of use, thus leading to modifications in collection development policies in order to increase the relevance of the collection to the needs of the users. Another possible objective is to identify little used items so that they can be relegated to less accessible (and less costly) storage areas, or even discarded completely.

The fact that one might modify a collection development policy, affecting future acquisitions, implies that present patterns of use can be taken to be good predictors of future use. Line and Sandison (1974) have contended that such assumptions are unjustifiable, but present no data to support this claim. On the other hand, in a classic study at the University of Chicago, Fussler and Simon (1969) collected evidence to suggest that past use is a good indicator of present use and, therefore, present use may well be a good predictor of future use. Newhouse and Alexander (1972) support this view, which appears entirely reasonable because of the considerable inertia likely to exist in a large community of users. In the academic community, reading lists do change, new courses emerge, others disappear; sometimes completely new programs are established or existing ones discontinued. Nevertheless, changes occurring from year to year have only a minor effect on the overall patterns of need and demand; a few things change but much more remains the same. The same is true of the public library community. Unless some quite unpredictable event suddenly occurs—such as a huge and unexpected influx of some ethnic minority into the community—changes in the composition and interests of the population will occur very gradually. In the industrial environment, sudden changes of direction for the organization, as a result perhaps of a merger or the sale of a subsidiary, are somewhat more common. Even here, however, they are the exception rather than the rule.

It seems entirely reasonable to suppose, then, that one can learn much about a collection from a study of what is now being borrowed from it. This chapter will consider the use of circulation data in the evaluation of a collection.

General Patterns of Use

It has long been conjectured, and more recently demonstrated, that the pattern of use of books in a library follows a hyperbolic distribution—a rather small number of items accounts for a large proportion of all the uses and the majority of items are little if ever used. The situation is illustrated in Exhibit 6, where percentage of circulation is plotted against percentage of collection. According to this diagram, while all the collection is needed to account for all of the use, it appears that about 60% of the use is accounted for by only about 10% of the collection, and 80% of the use seems to come from about 20% of the collection.

The hyperbolic distribution of Exhibit 6 has been shown to apply to a wide variety of activities involving human selection from a finite number of possibilities (for a complete discussion see Fairthorne, 1969). The use of words in a language (Zipf, 1935) and the scatter of periodical articles over periodical titles (Bradford, 1948)—most human communication is accounted for by a very small number of the words available, most articles on a subject are concentrated in a very small nucleus of highly productive periodicals—are distributions that resemble Exhibit 6 when the data are presented as cumulative percentages. In many cases it has been found that about 80% of use comes from about 20% of the items (whatever they happen to be—words, books, airlines, consumer products), which led to the idea of an "80/20" rule. However, this is nothing more than a rough rule of thumb. While the pattern of use of any book collection will follow a hyperbolic distribution, such as Exhibit 6, the steepness of the curve is likely to vary from one institution to the next. Thus, in library A, 80% of use may come from 20% of the collection while in B it may come from 45%.

Before automation was applied to record-keeping activities in libraries, the analysis of circulation was based upon the drawing of samples. As described by Jain (1967), two approaches were possible: the collection sample and the checkout sample. The former involves the selection of a random sample of items from the entire collection or from selected subject areas, usually through use of the shelf list, locating the books involved and plotting their circulation history from the earliest use to the present. This was the method used by Fussler and Simon

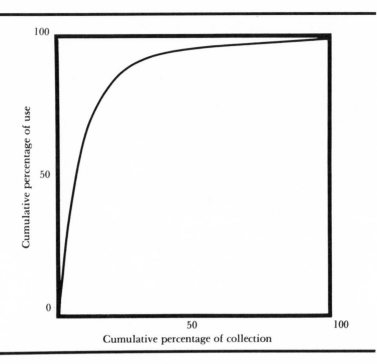

Exhibit 6

Distribution of use of items in a collection

(1969). Clearly, the method will only work if every book carries a card or slip recording the dates of each use. The main purpose of this approach is to determine the rate of obsolescence of the collection in various subject fields—that is, the rate at which use declines with the age of the materials.

The checkout sample, on the other hand, involves the analysis of all items borrowed during a particular period of time—say three selected months during the year. It is used mostly to study the subject distribution of circulation, although it can also yield an estimate of rate of obsolescence when publication dates of items borrowed are analyzed (see Chapter 6).

With automated circulation systems, however, the need for sampling disappears; data can be gathered as a continuous byproduct of the operation of the system. Records representing all circulations rather than a sample can be manipulated by computer program to produce data on subject distribution of the circulation, to identify the most heavily used titles, and (if the data are collected for a sufficiently long period) to measure rate of obsolescence.*

The use of automated systems permits an analysis of circulation patterns based upon large amounts of data collected over a considerable period of time. The most complete study of this type was performed on circulation data for 86 months gathered at the Hillman Library of the University of Pittsburgh (Kent et al., 1979).

The Pittsburgh study gives us the best data available to support the pattern of use illustrated in Exhibit 6. The data are as follows:

Percentage of circulation	Percentage of collection circulating at all	Number of items borrowed
20	4	11,593
40	12	33,081
60	23	64,584
80	42	121,018
100	100	285,373

These data are a little misleading because they are based solely on items borrowed during the 86 month period. Approximately half the items in the collection of the Hillman Library were not borrowed at all during this period. To get the relationship between circulation and items owned, then, the values in the center column above can be roughly halved. In other words, 20% of the circulation comes from only 2% of the collection, 40% from about 6% of the collection, and so on. Interestingly enough, the Pittsburgh data conform closely to the 80/20 rule.

Even more interesting, perhaps, are the data showing frequency of use of individual titles, as follows:

Number of circulations per year	Number of titles
1	63,526
2	25,653
3	11,855
4	6,055
5	3,264
6	1,727
7	931
8	497

---

*An "off the shelf" circulation system, of course, may not have these features built into it.

Of those titles that circulate at all during a year, more than half circulate only once; the number that circulate frequently are very few indeed. Moreover, these data show a remarkably regular linear decline: the number of items circulating twice is almost half the number circulating once, the number circulating three times is approximately half the number circulating twice, and so on (see Exhibit 7).

By looking at the circulation data for a group of books acquired in a particular time period, Kent and his colleagues concluded that about 40% of the books added to the Hillman Library had not been borrowed even once in the first six years after they were acquired, and many others had been used only once or twice. If one applied a very modest "cost-effectiveness criterion" of two circulations or more during the lifetime of a book in the library, about 54% of the items should not have been added (i.e., only 46% circulate two or more times). If the criterion was three or more circulations, about 62% of the items should not have been added.

As one might expect, these findings shocked many people and many were inclined to disbelieve. Nevertheless, similar results have since been obtained in much smaller academic libraries. For example, Hardesty (1981) took a sample of 1,904 books acquired during a six-month period by a small liberal arts college and tracked their circulations for a period of five years. The data are as follows:

Number of circulations	Items circulating this many times in first 3 years after acquisition		Items circulating this many times in first 5 years after acquisition	
	Number	%	Number	%
0	843	44.3	702	36.9
1-5	911	47.8	951	49.9
6-10	118	6.2	166	8.7
11+	32	1.7	85	4.5

These data are not too different from those collected at Pittsburgh. About 44% of the items acquired had not circulated at all after 3 years and 37% had not circulated at all after 5 years. The average number of circulations per book after 3 years was only 1.7 and then rose to only 2.4 after 5 years. The data collected by Ettelt (1978) in a small community college library are compatible with those of Hardesty and Kent et al. In most subjects, less than 50% of the books were found to circulate.

Some librarians argue that the fact that a book has not been used so far does not necessarily mean that it will never be used. While this is

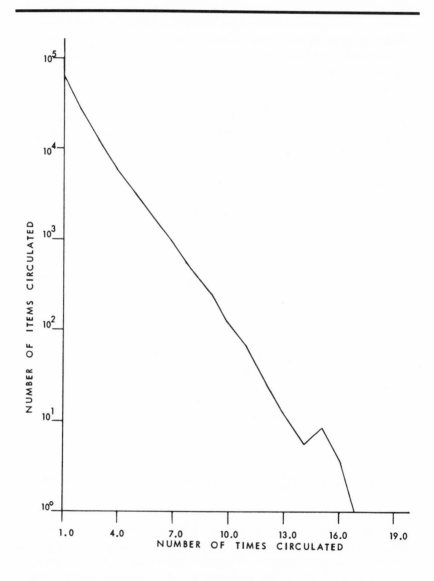

Exhibit 7

Distribution of circulation from University of
Pittsburgh study. Reprinted from Kent et al. (1979)
by courtesy of Marcel Dekker Inc.

true, it is important to recognize that the longer a book goes without being used the less probable it becomes that it will ever be used. The Pittsburgh data indicate that, when a book is added to the collection, there is little more than one chance in two (1/2) that it will ever be used. If it has not been used after the first two years in the library, the chance that it will ever be used drops to 1/4. If it has not been used after the first six years in the library, the probability that it will ever be used plummets to 1/50.*

Looked at another way, suppose that 5,000 books added to the collection of a library in 1980 have not been used up to the end of 1986 (i.e., after about 6 years in the library). The data from Pittsburgh suggest that only about 1/50 of these books—100 or so—will ever be used, however long they are retained. An important question for the library to consider is whether or not one can justify retaining 5,000 items for a possible use factor of 1/50.

The measure of "use" discussed so far in this chapter is circulation. Obviously, some books can be used in the library without being borrowed. Total use, then, exceeds recorded circulation. The in-house use of collections is discussed in Chapter 4.

Relative Use

The most obvious application of circulation data is to produce analyses of use of the collection by subject according to the various subdivisions of the classification scheme in use in the library. The Pittsburgh data are again of interest here for they show that, in terms of subject distribution, circulation records for only a few days give results remarkably close to those gathered for the whole period of 86 months. This provides some evidence for the "inertia" mentioned earlier: patterns of use of the collection change very slowly.

It was apparently Jain (1965-1969) who first pointed out that librarians should be less concerned with establishing the absolute use of portions of a collection than with determining "relative" use. What this really means is that one should use circulation data to reveal differences between actual and "expected" (in a probabilistic sense) behavior. Suppose, for example, that books on physics occupy 12% of a particular collection. Probability alone suggests that physics books should

---

*However, in studies performed at a university library in England, Taylor (see Urquhart and Urquhart, 1976) discovered that the proportion of previously unused books that became used was much the same whether the books had been unused for six or for fifteen years. At least, this was true for physics, politics, and English literature. In medicine the length of the disuse had a more marked effect.

account for 12% of the circulation. If they do, that portion of the collection is behaving exactly as expected. On the other hand, if physics books account for only 8% of the circulation, one can say that the class is "underused" (used less than expected) whereas it would be "overused" if it accounts for, say, 15% of all circulation.*

If data on the library's holdings in various classes are built into an automated circulation system, printouts can be generated to show for each class what proportion of the collection it occupies and what proportion of the circulation it accounts for. An example is given in Exhibit 8.

| | Collection | | Circulation | |
Class	Number of books	% of collection	Number of items borrowed	% of circulation
610	172	.17	65	.45
620	309	.31	48	.33
630	524	.52	27	.19
640	602	.60	73	.52
650	144	.14	35	.25

Exhibit 8

Hypothetical "relative use" data for selected
subdivisions of Dewey class 600

It is obvious from this table that circulation in 620 and 640 is close to what probability suggests it should be, while classes 610 and 650 are heavily overused and 630 is heavily underused. An automated circulation system could be used to generate such data in a more useful format. In particular, the system can identify those classes that deviate most from the expected behavior—those most overused and those most underused (see Dowlin and Magrath, 1983, for an example based on public library circulation).

The assumption is that the most deviant classes are those that need most attention. The circulation data merely highlight the deviant classes; they do not tell the librarian how to deal with them. One could argue that both overused and underused classes may fail to meet user

---

*An overused class is one in which items are used more than expected (in a probabilistic sense) relative to the proportion of the collection occupied by that class. An underused class is one in which items are used less than expected relative to the proportion of the collection occupied by that class.

needs. If a class is heavily overused (true of 610 in Exhibit 8 which gets almost three times the expected volume of use), the implication is that the library lacks the strength in this area to meet the present volume and variety of demands. The more overused a class, the lower the probability that any particular book will be on the shelf when looked for by a user. Moreover, the more overused the class, the less valuable it will be to the browser because of the phenomenon of "shelf bias."

Shelf bias is best illustrated through a simple example. Consider a brand new branch of a public library. The library has two shelves of books devoted to a popular subject, say personal computers (Exhibit 9). A user enters the new library shortly after it opens. He browses among the personal computer books and decides to borrow those that are most appealing. A second user enters the library an hour later. There is still a good selection of personal computer books available, although not quite as good as before, and this user leaves the library happy. As the day wears on, however, the selection of books available becomes less and less interesting as shelf bias increases. Shelf bias, then, refers to the fact that, all other things being equal, the shelves of an open-access library will tend to display books that nobody wants to borrow. The phenomenon was identified explicitly by Buckland (1972) and Buckland and Hindle (1969), who referred to it as "collection bias." This author prefers "shelf bias" because it seems more descriptive of what is actually taking place. Buckland (1975) expresses the bias in terms of the proportion of the material absent from the shelves at a particular time. Thus, if 80 books out of 240 were absent, the bias would be 33%.

A heavily underused class may be just as disturbing as one heavily overused. The class appears not to be of much interest to the community. This may reflect changing interests over time. On the other hand, it may indicate that the selection of books is just not a good one. Perhaps the library is buying the wrong books (e.g., too technical or too theoretical) or that it owns too many books that are out-of-date and should be discarded. It is possible that use of the class would increase substantially if it were thoroughly weeded and more attractive, up-to-date items added.

As stated earlier, circulation data can do little more than bring "problem" classes to the librarian's attention. It is then the librarian's task to look more closely at such classes in order to decide why they are behaving as they are and what corrective action appears to be necessary.

The degree of discrepancy between holdings and circulation can be expressed in several ways. The simplest, perhaps, is the "circulation/inventory ratio" (C/I) used by Wenger et al. (1979), which is nothing more than the number of circulations occurring in a class during a particular

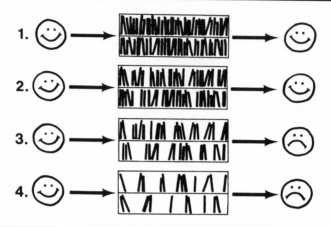

Exhibit 9

The phenomenon of shelf bias

period of time divided by the number of items in that class. Thus, a class with 7 items and 20 circulations receives a C/I ratio of 2.9 (20/7).* Dowlin and Magrath (1983) also use this but refer to it as an "inventory use ratio." "Stock turnover rate" is another term sometimes used. Nimmer (1980) has used the measure "intensity of circulation"— number of circulations per 100 titles held.

Bonn (1974) proposed a simple "use factor" (renamed as "degree of use" by Gillentine et al., 1981), which is the proportion (or percentage) of the circulation accounted for by a class divided by the proportion of the collection occupied by that class. With this type of ratio, as used by Jenks (1976), the higher the figure the greater the overuse. For example, a class accounting for 3.49% of the collection and 4.79% of the circulation receives a score of 137.25 while one that accounts for .36% of the collection but only .16% of the circulation gets a score of 44.44. Metz (1983) refers to this measure as the "proportional use statistic" and Aguilar (1986) as "percentage of expected use." Aguilar derived his use of this measure from Mills (1982).

---

*They also suggest the introduction of a time variable, incorporating in the equation the number of days the library was open during the period represented by the use data. Thus

$$\frac{20 \text{ circulations}}{(7 \text{ books}) \times (64 \text{ days})}$$ yields a figure of 0.00446 circulations per book per day.

Trochim et al. (1980) use the *difference* between holdings percentage and collection percentage for each class as an indicator of overuse or underuse. Mills (1982) is critical of this: a difference of 0.2 would apply equally to a subject occupying 0.5% of the collection and getting 0.7% of the use as it would to one occupying 2.5% of the collection and getting 2.7% of use, yet the proportional discrepancy between holdings and use is very much greater for the smaller class.

Mostyn (1974) uses the term "supply-demand equality" in referring to the relative use relationship; an overused class is one in which demand exceeds supply and vice versa for an underused class.

In order to make informed decisions, the librarian should have more than the relative use data available. It would also be important to know, for any particular class, what the level of current purchasing is and whether use of the class is increasing or decreasing over time. Consider the following hypothetical data that could be generated from a management information system within a library:

Class	% of collection	% of current acquisitions	% of circulation	Latest year's circulation compared with previous year (%)
y	2.8	3.5	0.2	−15

Class y is very much underused and use continues to decline. This would appear to be a class in which interest is waning and it seems hard to justify the fact that 3.5% of all acquisitions fall in an area that accounts for only 0.2% of current circulation. Similar data for other classes could lead to quite different conclusions. For example, if a class is underused and on the decline but percentage of current acquisitions is well below percentage of collection, the situation seems to have righted itself and no further action is called for.

The more useful data the librarian has available, the more likely it is that collection development decisions will be made wisely. In a coordinated collection development program for Illinois libraries (Krueger, 1983), the following data were collected by each participating library for each subject area of the collection: percentage of collection occupied, percentage of use accounted for, percentage of interlibrary loan requests accounted for, percentage of current acquisitions, percentage of current American publishing output (from *Publishers Weekly* and the *Bowker Annual*), median age of materials used, median age of materials owned, and an "availability" percentage (based on sampling to determine what percentage of books owned in that class was actually available on the shelf when sought). An example of the data collected is shown in Exhibit 10.

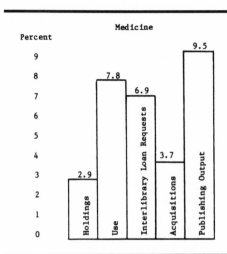

Median age of materials circulated and used in-house is the highest of all subjects (1976). Median age of holdings is 1966–70.
Availability – 69%

Exhibit 10

Sample of complementary data collected to evaluate
the "medicine" collection of a library. Reproduced from Krueger (1983)
by permission of the Illinois State Library

The librarian should look at fine circulation data rather than coarse to avoid jumping to the wrong conclusions. The fact that Dewey class 640 is overused does not necessarily mean that the entire class is overused; it may be that only the cookbooks are overused and all other subdivisions are actually underused. Likewise, overuse of Library of Congress class QA may suggest the need for strengthening of the entire mathematics collection when, in fact, it is only the computer science books that are affecting the results. Trochim et al. (1980) provide detailed instructions on gathering relative use data by taking circulation samples and either (a) stack samples or (b) shelflist samples.*

While automated circulation systems can be used to generate more and better data than any previously available, they are not essential to

*All three samples can be considered to have some bias. Clearly, circulation samples are biased toward the more popular items while stack samples and shelflist samples are biased toward less used items. For certain types of analysis such biases may not be important. For other types of analysis, they might be. For example, a shelflist sample is inappropriate for use in an *availability* study because it will contain too many items unlikely to be in demand.

the type of analysis discussed in this chapter. Before computers were applied in libraries at all, McClellan (1956) adopted an ingenious technique for monitoring use of a collection in a public library. On one selected day each month, he had members of his staff perform a count of the number of books on the shelf and the number in circulation for each subdivision of the classification scheme. The data thus collected would look as follows:

Class	On shelf	In circulation
610	128	44
620	200	109
630	321	203
640	501	101
650	89	55

These figures can serve the same purpose as the relative use figures discussed earlier. They can be converted into percentage use factors. In the case of class 650, 38% of the collection (55/144) was in use when this sample was taken, whereas only 17% of class 640 was in use.

Once more, the most deviant classes can be identified by this procedure. The hypothetical data presented, for example, suggest that considerable shelf bias may exist in class 650 but much less in 640 or 610. McClellan was able to use this method to identify classes requiring attention and then to observe the effects of his actions over a period of time—e.g., the effect of a drastic weeding of one of the subclasses or the effect of a large influx of new books. He also used the method as a key factor in allocating the book budget over the various classes. Clearly, the data collected clerically by McClellan could be generated automatically by computer. That is, if holdings data are recorded in a circulation system, printouts can be produced for any selected day to show the proportion of each subclass on loan at that time.

Last Circulation Date

Trueswell (1964-1969) has used and described an ingenious procedure for estimating what proportion of the collection accounts for what proportion of the use or, more importantly, to identify *which* books account for a specified proportion of the use. The "last circulation date" (LCD) method requires that one collect only two dates: the date on which a book is borrowed in a current circulation period and the date on which it was last previously borrowed. Suppose, for example, that "current circulation period" is defined as all books borrowed in January

1987. For each book borrowed on January 2, this date is recorded along with the date on which this book was last previously borrowed (as recorded on date slip or book card), and likewise for January 3, 4, and so on. At the end of the month of data gathering, current circulation percentages can be plotted against the time elapsing since items were last previously borrowed, as shown in Exhibit 11.

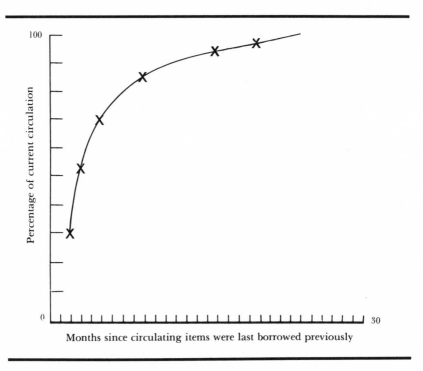

Exhibit 11

Plot of results from last circulation date method

The hypothetical data of Exhibit 11 can be interpreted as follows: about 30% of current circulation is accounted for by books that were borrowed at least once in the month immediately preceding the current circulation, about 50% were borrowed in the preceding two months, and so on. It appears from the diagram that about 90% of the use is accounted for by items last previously borrowed within the preceding 14 months.

If one removed from the shelves of the library all books that have not circulated within the last 14 months, the books remaining there can be expected to account for about 90% of future circulations. The method can thus be used to establish a cut-off for retiring portions of the collection to less accessible storage areas or to identify a "core" collection likely to account for a specified percentage of future use—the 90% library, the 95% library, or whatever. Trueswell, in fact, has used the method to identify the volumes that should appear in a 99% library. In one academic library this was found to be 40% of the collection (i.e., 40% would account for 99% of the circulation); in a second it was found to be a mere 25% of the collection.

Underlying the LCD method is the fact that most books now being borrowed were previously borrowed in the fairly recent past and very few books are now borrowed that have sat unused on the shelves for a long period of time. This has been confirmed in a number of different ways, perhaps most dramatically by Metz (1980):

> At the Virginia Polytechnic Institute and State University, a collection of over one million volumes, a "rolling" or "on the fly" conversion to brief machine readable circulation records was in place for only *four-and-a-half months* before the probability that an item being brought to the circulation desk would already have been entered in the system reached .50. Only some 57,000 items had been entered in the system at this halfway point. (Pages 29-30)

Slote (1982) uses the term "shelf-time period" to refer to the length of time a book remains on the shelf between circulations.* He describes a number of methods that can be used to gather shelf-time data, depending largely on the type of circulation system in use. The shelf-time approach is essentially the same as the LCD approach. Slote claims that reliable shelf-time data for a collection can be obtained from as few as 500 consecutive circulation transactions.

In applying the LCD method, one would obviously have to exclude from consideration books added only recently to the library—e.g., books acquired within the past two years but not circulated, when books not circulated within the last 48 months are to be retired. In a study at the University of Wisconsin, Oshkosh, Sargent (1979) applied the LCD method and discovered that 99% of the circulation came from items that had circulated at least once in the preceding 7 1/2 years. Random samples drawn from the shelf list and catalogs, however, showed that, in this young and rapidly growing library, 56% of the collection would be needed to account for 99% of the circulation. It seems, then, that the LCD

---

*In actual fact, a distinction is made between "closed-end" and "open-end" shelf time. The former is the time elapsing between the last two recorded circulations while the latter is the time between the last circulation and the date the observation is made. Williams (1986) gives a useful account of the application of the Slote method.

method will be more applicable in identifying a "core" in a relatively old library than it will in a very new one.

The most comprehensive application of the LCD method has been described by Trochim et al. (1980), who present results for various subject fields derived from data gathered in three college libraries.

Title Availability

So far in this chapter aggregate circulation date—e.g., on books in some subject area—have been discussed rather than data on individual titles. It is clear, however, that an automated circulation system can provide data on the use made of particular titles and can "flag" titles that are now so heavily used that additional copies should be purchased or some other steps taken to improve their availability. This aspect of evaluation will be discussed fully in Chapter 8.

Interlibrary Loan Analysis

Another approach to collection evaluation involves the examination of interlibrary loan (ILL) requests generated within a library. The justification for this is obvious: if a library is borrowing heavily in some subject field this probably indicates that the library's own holdings on this subject need to be strengthened.

Byrd et al. (1982) have described a method for determining strengths and weaknesses in a collection based on the difference in proportions between the subject breakdown of a library's acquisitions and the subject breakdown of the interlibrary loan requests it generates. The theory is that the classes needing greatest attention are those in which the volume of materials borrowed most exceeds the volume of materials purchased. This discrepancy is expressed as a "collection balance indicator" (CBI), a relative percentage, as follows:

$$100 \times \frac{\text{New acquisitions in this class}}{\text{Total acquisitions}} - \frac{\text{Titles borrowed in this class}}{\text{Total titles borrowed}}$$

A positive value on the CBI indicates a subject area relatively strong in terms of current acquisitions while a negative value indicates one relatively weak. This can be illustrated through two simple examples:

$$1. \quad 100 \times \frac{100}{400} - \frac{12}{120} = 15$$

$$2. \quad 100 \times \frac{40}{400} - \frac{30}{120} = -15$$

In the first case, 25% of the acquisitions are made in this subject field but only 10% of the titles borrowed fall in this area. The CBI is a high 15. The second case puts the proportions exactly in reverse—10% of acquisitions and 25% of titles borrowed—and the value is a low -15.

Aguilar (1984) performed a monumental study of the relationship between internal circulation and interlibrary loan requests based on about 86,000 ILL transactions and almost two million circulation records from eighteen Illinois libraries. He found support for his hypothesis that a class that is overused (as defined earlier in this chapter) in a library will be a class in which the library will borrow many items, whereas underused classes tend not to generate large numbers of ILL requests. This supports the assumption made earlier in this chapter that it is overused classes rather than underused classes that are most in need of strengthening.

Collection/Curriculum Comparisons

A number of investigators have attempted to determine the adequacy of the collections of an academic library by comparing the holdings with "classified" course descriptions. While somewhat different from the other methods described in this chapter, the method is sufficiently related to be worth considering here.

Using the classification scheme by which books are arranged on the library's shelves, classification numbers are assigned to all of the course descriptions appearing in the catalog of a university. This "profile" of academic interests can then be matched against the subject profile of library holdings (as reflected in the shelf list), of current acquisitions, or of circulation.

Examples of use of such techniques can be found in the work of McGrath, Golden, and Jenks. McGrath (1968) was able to show, for each academic department, the number of circulated books relevant to the departmental profile, the percentage of the total circulation accounted for by these books, the enrollment for the department, and a circulation/enrollment ratio. Golden (1974) related the class numbers associated with a course to the number of books owned in these classes and to enrollment figures for the course in an attempt to identify strengths and weaknesses in the collection. Jenks (1976) compared circulation figures with the number of students in each department and with the number of books matching the profile of each department. He also ranked departments according to the use each made of that part of the collection matching its interest profile.

Power and Bell (1978) propose a more elaborate formula that takes into account, for each academic department, the number of faculty members, the number of students at various levels, the holdings matching departmental profile, and circulation.

McGrath (1972) has shown that books matching the profile of institutional interests are much more likely to be borrowed than books not matching the profile, while McGrath et al. (1979) have used a subject classification approach to determine to what extent graduate and undergraduate students borrow books outside their own disciplines.

Evans and Beilby (1983) describe collection evaluation through a sophisticated management information system employed within the libraries of the State University of New York. In one machine-readable file are stored student enrollment data classified by subject field according to the Higher Education General Information Survey (HEGIS) codes. By using OCLC tapes, together with a conversion tape showing equivalencies between the HEGIS codes and Library of Congress class numbers, it is possible to relate the acquisitions data of a library to the enrollment. Thus, for each HEGIS code (e.g., 1103, German language), the system will generate a printout showing the number of titles acquired by the library, the percentage of the total acquisitions that this represents, the number of student credit hours, and the percentage of the total credit hours that this represents. Subject areas in which strong (or weak) relationships exist between student credit hours and acquisitions patterns can thus be identified, and any necessary corrections made.

Spaulding and Stanton (1976) and Kennedy (1983) describe the use of the Dewey Decimal Classification (DDC) as an aid to book selection in an industrial library network. A selection profile for each member library is constructed, using DDC numbers plus verbal descriptions. Circulation data were used in the building of the profiles. Computer-generated reports allow a manager to determine to what extent materials purchased in a particular time period match a library's profile.

Gabriel (1987) has described the use of keyword searching in online data bases, in place of the use of class numbers, to assess the coverage of a collection. Keywords associated with course descriptions are used to identify items relevant to each course.

This chapter has mostly dealt with the use of circulation and related data in collection evaluation. Circulation data, however, have two obvious limitations:

1. They tell nothing about use of materials within the library.
2. They represent successes (a book borrowed is one that a user considers at least sufficiently interesting to take from the library) but reveal nothing about failures. Put differently, number of books borrowed is not an indicator of *success rate*.

The first of these limitations is dealt with in Chapter 4 and the second in Chapter 8.

Study Questions

1. You have recently been appointed Director of a public library serving a community of 100,000. After two months on the job you have come to the conclusion that the nonfiction collection is very unbalanced. Looking around at the shelves, you feel that some subject areas are over-represented—the collection is too strong for the needs of the community—while others seem completely inadequate. At the moment, however, this is just a suspicion. What data would you collect, over what period of time, in order to identify over-represented and under-represented subject areas, and how would you go about collecting these data? Unfortunately, the library does not have an automated circulation system.

2. You are the librarian of a small liberal arts college. A new automated circulation system is to be installed and you can now specify the data to be collected by this system. For purposes of collection development and management, which data will you collect and how will you make use of these data?

4. In-House Use

Circulation data do not give a complete picture of a collection because they fail to take into account the use of materials within the library. This may not be too important in the case of a public library, but it is in a research library, where in-house use may greatly exceed circulation. A number of critics have attacked the studies performed at the University of Pittsburgh (Kent et al., 1979) on the grounds that they come to conclusions about use of the collection that are based largely on circulation data (see, for example, Borkowski and Macleod, 1979; Schad, 1979; Voigt, 1979).

Nevertheless, if one excludes items that are not allowed to leave the library, there is no real reason to suppose that the items used within a library will be much different from those borrowed. Indeed, evidence exists to suggest that the books used in a library are more or less the same as those borrowed. McGrath (1971), for example, discovered a strong correlation between the subject matter of books borrowed and those used within the library, while Fussler and Simon (1969) found that the proportional use of parts of the collection was similar whether circulation or in-house use was considered (e.g., if physics materials are borrowed twice as much as chemistry materials they will tend to be used in the library twice as much). More recently, Hardesty (1981) reported a study in a small liberal arts college in which:

> ...each book had to be physically examined, and it soon became evident that books with no recorded circulation also had remained virtually untouched within the library. Their pages were unsmudged and their spines creaked as they were opened. (Page 265)

Other evidence on the correlation between circulation and in-house use is presented by Bommer (1973) and Domas (1978). Using questionnaires placed in randomly selected monographs and bound volumes of periodicals, Lawrence and Oja (1980) discovered a statistically significant but weak correlation between the number of times a volume circulates and the number of inhouse uses it receives. Hindle and Buckland (1978) point out that:

> Books that circulate little get relatively little in-house use and the higher the circulation the higher the level of in-library use. (Page 270)

In a small academic library in England, Harris (1977) found that about 18% of the collection accounted for all in-library use, about 45% of the collection accounted for all circulation, and about 51% of the collection accounted for *all* use. In other words, only an additional 6% of the collection was needed, beyond the circulating portion, to account for all use (see Exhibit 12). As discussed later, Harris's criterion for in-house use was much more relaxed than that most frequently employed in libraries.

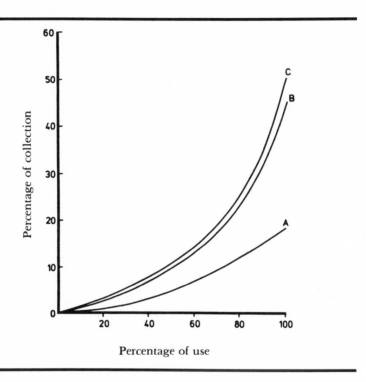

Exhibit 12

Proportion of collection needed to account for all in-house use (A), all circulation (B) and total use (C). Reprinted from Harris (1977) by permission of Aslib and the author

In the Pittsburgh studies it was estimated that about 75% of the materials used in-house had also circulated. Assuming that a reasonable proportion of the 25% that had not circulated consisted of materials that are considered "noncirculating," it would appear that very few of the items used in the library had not also circulated.

Hayes (1981), on the other hand, performed a mathematical analysis of data from the Pittsburgh studies which, he claims, reveals that circulation is not an adequate indicator of total use.

The most obvious difference between a measure of in-house use and the measure of circulation is the ambiguity of the former. A book either is or is not borrowed, but what constitutes a "use" within a library? If a book is removed from the shelves, casually glanced at and immediately returned, has it been "used?" If it is removed, some portion of it read at the shelves, and it is then put back, has it been used? If it is carried to a table, along with others, glanced at and pushed to one side, has it been used?

One cannot be certain that any item is used "substantively" within a library without interviewing representative users or, at least, observing them, and neither procedure is very practical except on an extremely limited scale. On the other hand, circulation figures reflect only the activity of *borrowing* and tell us nothing about level or type of use. It is quite possible that substantial numbers of items borrowed receive no significant level of use.

The easiest way to find out what items or types of items are consulted in the library is to examine materials left on tables or desks, and this is the method most frequently used. For a particular period of time (at Pittsburgh, 30 sample days, one per week for 30 weeks) such materials are collected at regular intervals each day—say, 10 AM, 2 PM, 7 PM, and 10 PM—their identities are recorded, and they are then returned to the shelf. To ensure that, as far as possible, this procedure records all in-house uses, the library should implement an all-out "cooperation campaign." Signs prominently placed in the library will urge users not to reshelve materials they consult. These can be supplemented by notices in library bulletins, cards handed to users entering the library on the days selected for the survey, or any other procedure that seems likely to work in a particular institution.

"Table counts" of this type can be used to identify specific materials used within a library, allowing categorizations by subject, type of document, age of material, or other characteristics of interest, depending on what data are recorded before items are reshelved.

This method of measuring in-house use has been criticized on a number of counts, including:
1. However strongly one pleads, some users will reshelve materials so the method will give an underestimate of actual use.
2. Some types of users are more likely to reshelve than others so the method gives a distorted picture of actual use.
3. Some books left on tables may be used more than once while others may not have been used at all.
4. Whether books are carried to tables, or left there after use, may be influenced by physical characteristics (e.g., very heavy books may be more likely to be taken to a table but less likely to be reshelved).

The first of these criticisms is valid: total use will be underestimated. By placing "slips" in a sample of books in such a way that the slip cannot remain undisturbed if the book is removed from the shelf, Harris (1977) estimated that the complete use of materials in-house may be as much as 20 times the use reflected in materials left on tables. Clearly, Harris is saying that a book removed from the shelf, however briefly, is a book used. Lawrence and Oja (1980), using a similar technique, estimated that collection use in two University of California libraries may be six times greater than suggested by circulation data alone.

Also, using a technique similar to if not identical with that used by Harris,* Taylor discovered that about 22% of all volumes of periodicals consulted in a large academic library were left on tables (see Urquhart and Urquhart, 1976). By specifically asking users to leave things on tables, he was able to raise this figure to 41%.

One can readily accept the fact that a count of materials left on tables will in some way underestimate amount of in-house use. However, it is not clear why this should be considered important. The purpose of performing an in-house study should be to discover *what* is being used, not *how much* the library is being used. Common sense suggests that, as with circulation, in-house use is heavily skewed so that most of it comes from a very small part of the collection. If the sampling period is long enough, then, the fact that some things are reshelved may not affect one's conclusions about what is being used in the library and at what levels. To take a concrete example, if 5 people reshelve volumes of the *Journal of Applied Physics* and 20 others do not, table counts give an underestimate of use of this item but still indicate that it is heavily used in comparison with many other physics journals which may have recorded only one or two uses over the same period.

If one *must* arrive at an estimate of total in-house use, it is possible to do so by means of "observation periods." For certain blocks of time during the sampling period, selected at random, users of the library are discreetly observed to find how many reshelve volumes and how many do not. Suppose one observes 100 users in this way. They remove 350 volumes from the shelves, leave 200 on tables, and reshelve 150. If this is a representative sample of all users, one can conclude that volumes left on tables represent approximately 57% (200/350) of all uses (Wenger and Childress, 1977).**

---

*The slip used by Taylor (1977) is illustrated in Exhibit 13.

**It should be recognized, however, that observation of this kind is not easily achieved and that a staff member may feel "uncomfortable" in trying to observe library users unobtrusively.

The second major criticism of table counts—that certain types of people are more likely to reshelve than others—rests on assumptions that have never been tested. Peat (1981), for example, claims that researchers—faculty and graduate students—are much more likely to reshelve than undergraduates but presents no evidence to support this.

Of course, there may exist certain factors within a particular library that could cause table counts to give serious distortions in terms of overall patterns of use. For example, the shelves devoted to subject *A* could be immediately adjacent to tables, while those devoted to *B* could be quite far from the nearest tables. One could argue, then, that *A* users are more likely than *B* users to carry things to tables. On the other hand, if *B* users go to the trouble ot taking things to tables, they may be more likely than *A* users to leave them there, so one factor might offset the other. Apart from factors of this type, influences associated with the layout of a library, one has no reason to suppose that (for example) economists are more likely to reshelve than metallurgists.

Unfortunately, when different methods of measuring in-house use are compared, they tend to give divergent results. A comprehensive study of in-house use of materials, involving the comparison of several methodologies in six public libraries of varying size, is reported by Rubin (1986). Questionnaires, interviews, and unobtrusive observation were all used, and counts were made of materials left on tables. Table counts indicated that two items were borrowed for every one item used in the library. However, library users who were interviewed claimed to use as many items in the library as they borrowed, while questionnaire data suggested that somewhat more items were used in the library than were borrowed (ratio of 1.2 to 1.0). Rubin recommends the questionnaire approach because it is relatively easy to administer yet is capable of collecting data on users as well as on materials used.

A library will usually do table counts for only a very limited period of time because of the resources needed to record data on items used before they are returned to the shelves. Shaw (1978, 1979), however, has described an ingenious method that would allow the use of a collection to be monitored continuously. In the "dotting method,"* rather than noting identifying details for a volume before it is returned to the shelf, the fact that it has been used is merely recorded by placing an adhesive "dot" on its spine. The dot, which can actually be shot onto the spine by a special type of "gun," is clearly visible when the volume is on the library shelves. If dots of different colors are used, one can distinguish items borrowed from items used in the library.

---

*Slote (1982) refers to it as the "spine-marking" method.

Obviously, every item must be given a dot before it is returned to the shelves, whether from circulation or in-house use. This will cause a lot of extra work for a few weeks after the procedure is first instituted. But dots are not put on items that already have them, and it will not be long before most items coming up for reshelving have already been dotted. After several months, the items needing a dot will be the exception rather than the rule so the procedure can go on indefinitely.

The beauty of this approach is that, merely by walking through the library, one can readily identify which volumes have been used (i.e., left on tables) and which not, including the earliest volumes of each periodical that have been used. Moreover, with different colors, one can identify items borrowed but not used in the library, items used in-house but not borrowed, items borrowed and used in-house, and items not used at all. Of course, the method does not reveal how frequently a particular item has been used. Nevertheless, if one is to believe the results of several published studies, it is enough to be able to identify the items that are not used at all.*

In studying use made of periodicals within a library, Taylor (1977) has gone beyond use per se and attempted to determine whether or not a reader found anything of value in a volume consulted. A survey form (see Exhibit 13) is placed in each volume. The user is asked to place this form in different colored folders depending on whether or not the volume was found to be of use. Because these forms are placed at known page numbers, Taylor claims that it is unlikely for a consultation to go undetected even if the user does not cooperate in the process.

The methods described so far collect anonymous data on in-house use—they show what is being used but not who is using it. Anonymity could be reduced through a survey form, such as the one used by Taylor, that asked users to indicate their departmental affiliation and status (undergraduate, master's student, doctoral student, faculty).

For more precise data, however, it would be necessary to interview a sample of people actually using materials in the library. Random sampling can be based on a seating pattern. Every chair in which a user could be seated is given an identifying number. Time slots for interviewing of users (selected times on selected days in selected weeks) are established. To each time slot a sequence of seat numbers is randomly assigned. An interviewer approaches the first seat thus identified. If a user is present there, the user is interviewed. If not, the interviewer proceeds to the next seat indicated, and so on until a user is located. The interview is conducted in order to discover relevant details on the user as

*For example, in a study of 804 journals received by an education/psychology library, Perk and Van Pulis (1977) found that 192 titles, 24%, were completely unused.

THIS LETTER FORMS PART OF A LIBRARY SURVEY

The librarian would very much appreciate your
help in carrying out a survey of periodicals used
within the library.

A.   IF YOU HAVE FOUND AN ARTICLE OR ARTICLES IN
      THIS VOLUME OF USE TO YOUR STUDIES OR RESEARCH
      please place this form in the RED FOLDER
      located at the end of the stack.

B.   IF YOU HAVE USED THIS VOLUME BUT DID NOT FIND
      ANY INFORMATION OF USE TO YOUR STUDIES OR
      RESEARCH please place this form in the BLUE
      FOLDER located at the end of the stack.

TITLE   *No 54*
        Per 6/2
YEAR
        17 '56

Exhibit 13

Survey form used by Taylor (1977) and how it is placed in bound volume of periodical.
Reprinted by permission of The Haworth Press

well as on the material being used. Procedures of this kind (see Daiute
and Gorman, 1974, for a detailed description) can yield data qualitatively different from the anonymous data, including identities of users,
correlations between users and uses (e.g., who uses bound periodicals,
who uses physics periodicals, how much use is made of physics materials by faculty and students in other departments), and an indication of
the extent to which the library's facilities are being used without con-
comitant use of library materials.

Study Questions

1. Black University has a consolidated Science Library serving all of the science faculties except that of medicine. Through an automated circulation system, it has excellent data on the use of its collections in terms of borrowings, but has no data at all on use of materials within the library. The Science Librarian suspects that the circulation data alone give a somewhat incomplete and distorted picture of the total use of the collections. She would like to do a one-time study of the in-house use of library materials. At the same time, she wants to know if it might somehow be possible to "calibrate" the in-house data to the circulation data so that, in the future, the circulation data can "predict" the distribution of in-house use. How should the study be conducted? What would you advise her on the calibration problem?

2. What are the advantages/disadvantages of knowing which volumes have been removed from the shelves of a library, however briefly, as opposed to which have been carried to tables?

3. The Undergraduate Library of a large university keeps issues of 300 periodicals in a prominent display area. For each title, the latest issue is displayed and back issues for the preceding six months are kept in adjacent storage space. Space has become a problem and it is now necessary to reduce this display to one-half of its present size. What data would you collect in order to make the best decision on how to use the reduced space? How would you collect these data?

5. Evaluation of Periodicals

In periods of austerity, when a library finds its budget for the purchase of materials to be shrinking, subscriptions to periodicals are likely to be examined to determine which titles may be discontinued.

Duplicate titles may be the first group looked at, especially in large academic libraries. If cuts are to be made, to what extent can one justify having several periodicals duplicated in departmental libraries devoted to, say, biology, the health sciences, and veterinary medicine? But duplication need not be the paramount criterion for cancelling a subscription: some titles may be heavily used in each of several locations while other titles, for which only one copy exists, may receive little or no use.

This suggests that use data should exert the most influence on cancellation decisions. Since periodicals do not circulate in many libraries, or circulate with many restrictions, the use data will have to come from some type of in-library survey as described in the previous chapter.

A major question to be considered in this chapter is whether or not data available from outside the library can substitute for actual use data in making effective decisions on which periodicals to discontinue. This could be quite important—a librarian required to reduce subscription costs by 10% might have no time to collect use data before some deadline imposed on him.

Ranking Criteria

In making cancellation decisions, it would be useful if one could produce a ranked list of titles (or several ranked lists according to discipline) reflecting retention priorities, the titles at the bottom being those one could discontinue with least disturbance to library users.

By what criteria can such rankings be arrived at? The following seem the most obvious:

1. By actual use data collected in the library.
2. By use data that have already been collected (and perhaps published) by another library. Urquhart and Urquhart (1976) suggest that, in some subject fields, periodical use data from the British Library Lending Division may closely parallel periodical use data collected in a British university.

3. By opinion. For example, members of the physics faculty are given a list of periodicals received by the physics library and asked to give each a score on a scale of 1 to 4, where 4 represents "essential" and 1 "of no interest." The periodicals are then ranked according to the sum of the scores received by each title. Some support for this approach is offered by Wenger and Childress (1977), who found that a periodical was very unlikely to be little used in the library when two or more scientists recommended it.

4. By citation. The *Journal Citation Reports* (JCR), published by the Institute for Scientific Information, rank periodicals in various subject fields according to the number of times they have been cited. These data are derived from the citation indexes published by the Institute.

5. Impact factor. This is another citation measure available from the JCR. The impact factor relates the number of citations received by a periodical to the number of articles published by that periodical (in a sense it is the citation equivalent of "relative use")—the more citations received per article published, the higher the impact factor. For example, if a journal published 20 articles in 1980-1985 and these received 448 citations in 1980-1987, the impact factor would be 22.4 (448/20).* Rankings based on impact factor and on simple citation counts will tend to differ: periodicals publishing only a few papers each year (e.g., those publishing review or survey articles) may have a low citation score but may have a high impact factor.

6. Cost-effectiveness. One of the "effectiveness" measures mentioned above (1-5) can be related to the cost of the periodical. If they are available, the library's own use data should be selected. The most cost-effective journals are those with lowest cost per use.**

7. By the number of articles contributed to a particular subject area. For example, Hafner (1976) used searches in MEDLARS to identify the most productive journals in various facets of nursing and Trubkin (1982) used a variety of data bases to identify the "core" periodicals in business and management. Seba and Forrest (1978) carried this further by using current awareness searches in data bases to identify

---

*Garfield (1986) distinguishes between *cited impact factor* and *total impact factor*. The latter relates number of citations to the total number of articles published by a journal in a particular period of time, while the former relates number of citations only to the number of articles published in a particular period *that were cited*.

**Holland (1976) describes a somewhat different cost-effectiveness measure. She takes into account how long a user would have to wait to obtain a photocopy from a periodical if it were not in the library's own collection. She is thus able to estimate the effects on "public service" of various levels of reduction in the budget.

the most relevant journals for the users of a special library. "Relevancy" was defined as the number of articles retrieved and judged relevant by users over the total number of articles published by a journal in a particular time period. The journals represented in the data base searches were compared with the library's holdings to identify nonproductive titles held as well as productive titles not held. The most "cost-effective" journals are those having the lowest cost per relevant article published.

There are many other ways in which journals can be ranked, including "exclusivity"—the proportion of all articles published by a journal that deal with some subject of interest (Hawkins, 1979), number of subscribers, and "influence" (Narin, 1976). However, the methods listed above would seem, at least on the surface, to be those most useful to the librarian in making practical decisions on which titles to discontinue.

Line (1978) has stated categorically that no external data (e.g., from citations or from another library) are of any value in predicting use within one's own library. He suggests that, if one compared ranked lists based on various criteria (e.g., the library's own use data, citation counts, data from another library, data based on user surveys) one might very well get similar rankings *at the top of the list.* That is, the same small set of, say, physics journals will be most used in all physics libraries, most cited, most highly favored by research workers, and so on. It is not necessary to gather any data to identify these titles—any physics librarian will know which they are.

For cancellation purposes, however, one is not interested in titles at the top of such a list but only in those at the bottom. As Line points out, ranked lists produced by the different criteria mentioned earlier are unlikely to be very similar at the bottom (journals consistently towards the bottom of all lists would have little reason to exist). Therefore, external data are of little use in making cancellation decisions.

Line's contentions make a great deal of sense. Consider Exhibit 14, which is a plot of use of periodicals in a hypothetical physics library. The distribution has been divided into three "zones" relating to degree of use in the library. Logic suggests that the titles in the first zone, most used in this library, will tend also to be most used in others, as well as being most cited and most often mentioned as important by physicists. As one moves into the later zones, however, this library's data can be expected to agree less and less with external data. Journals little used in this library will be used moderately or even heavily in others, this use varying with the different research interests of the parent institutions. Moreover, the least cited journals for a subject area as a whole will not necessarily be the least used in any particular library. Nor will they be the least cited if we narrow the subject field considerably. For example, certain journals dealing exclusively with irrigation may receive a low citation score for agriculture as a whole but they will be highly cited within the literature of irrigation and heavily used in institutions performing a significant level of irrigation research.

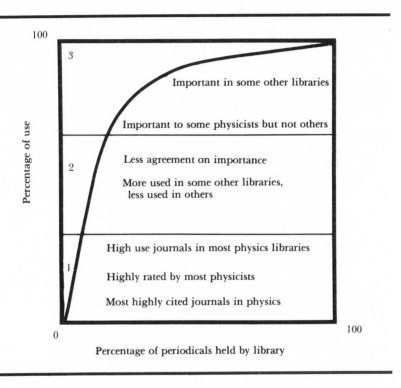

Exhibit 14

Plot of use versus percentage of periodicals
held by a hypothetical physics library

One is therefore inclined to agree with Line's contentions that ranked lists produced on the basis of different criteria are likely to be quite different at the bottom and that data external to the library may have little value to the librarian in making cancellation decisions. To what extent does evidence exist to support these contentions?

It has already been pointed out that rankings by impact factor are different from rankings by citation counts. One suspects that the titles at the top of the "opinion survey" list may contain a mixture of titles high on the citation count list and those high on the impact factor list. Top titles on the "use" list may also contain a mixture of high impact titles and high citation count titles.

The cost-effectiveness ranking will probably be quite different from all the others since it is the only one that takes cost into account. At the top of this list will be the high use titles that are relatively cheap. At the bottom will be the expensive titles that are little used. The middle of the list will include heavily used expensive titles and little used cheap ones, as well as some that are moderate on both scores.

In the field of physics, Scales (1976) has compared citation data from the *Journal Citation Reports* with use data derived from the British Library Lending Division (BLLD). Little agreement was found even at the top of the two lists: only one title was common to the five most used and five most cited and only sixteen were common to the first 50 titles on each list. A low correlation was also found between the 50 physics journals most used in the MIT Science Library and the BLLD use data. The correlation between the MIT data and the citation data was found to be slightly better than the correlation between the BLLD data and the citation data.

Pan (1978) gathered use data on 169 journals from six medical libraries, including use reflected in circulation, interlibrary loan and photocopying, as well as in-house use. These were compared with citation data from the *Journal Citation Reports*. She claimed to find a statistically significant correlation between a ranking of journals by use and a ranking by citation but no significant correlation between the use ranking and one based on impact factor. However, she also found that the size of a journal—in terms of number of articles published in a specified time period—or the number of subscribers to that journal correlated as well with the use rankings as did the citation rankings.*

In the field of sociology, Baughman (1974) claimed that citation studies could be used to predict "readership." Satariano (1978), however, found differences between Baughman's list of most cited journals in sociology and a list that 526 sociologists, selected by sampling 183 graduate departments, claimed to be "most read." Citation data underestimate use of popular journals and of specialty and regional journals in sociology. On the other hand, the most cited journals list includes

---

*Bennion and Karschamroon (1984) also found that number of subscribers correlated more closely with the results of an opinion survey than citation or any other bibliographic data did, which suggests that, if these data were readily available, they might be employed as a predictor of use in certain types of libraries.

some journals from related disciplines that do not appear among the list of titles most read.

Bennion and Karschamroon (1984) have compared the ranking of physics journals by "perceived usefulness" (based on a survey of 167 physicists) with rankings derived from multiple regression models incorporating several "bibliometric" values such as number of items published, citations received, impact factor, and ratio of citations made to citations received. These multivariate models are said to predict usefulness better than any single bibliometric predictor alone can do. The best single predictor was determined to be the number of subscribers to the journal.

Wiberley (1982), working in the field of social work, compared the rankings of journals derived from "national" citation data with rankings derived from "local" citation data. The national data were drawn from two leading journals and one specialized encyclopedia. The local data were the bibliographic references within publications of the faculty of a prominent school of social work. The local data were divided into two periods: 1971-1974 and 1975-1978. The national data were almost as good as the 1971-1974 local data in predicting the citation patterns of the 1975-1978 local data.

A number of other investigators have compared bibliometric data with use data or use data from one source with use data from another. There are too many to be reviewed comprehensively in this chapter. A useful summary is given by Broadus (1977).

Two other studies do deserve attention here. Stankus and Rice (1982) ranked journals by use data from an academic library (State University of New York at Albany) and compared this ranking with one based on citation counts and another based on impact factors. They found marked differences from one subject field to another. In biochemistry, excellent correlations throughout the lists were found, while in geoscience poor correlations occurred. In some fields, such as cell biology, a good correlation at the bottom of the list was discovered.

These results tend to suggest that there are some fields in which the programs of research and teaching at SUNYA are sufficiently different from the general "educational and scientific consensus" that citation is a poor predictor of use, whereas in other fields the SUNYA programs conform more closely to the general consensus. Stankus and Rice caution that use data are only likely to correlate with citation data if the use is reasonably heavy and not skewed by the eccentricities of a few frequent users.

Rice (1983) reports separately on another SUNYA study, this time in the field of chemistry. The ranking of periodicals by use in SUNYA libraries did not correlate particularly well with rankings based on *Journal Citation Reports* or the *Chemical Abstracts Service Source Index* (CASSI), the latter reflecting the number of periodical articles that various periodicals contribute to *Chemical Abstracts*. For example, *Industrial and Engineering Chemistry* ranks 14 in use at SUNYA but appears in position 66 on the JCR list and 770 on the CASSI list. On the other hand, two Russian journals appear among CASSI's top eight titles; by use at SUNYA, these rank in positions 85 and 86. Based on a survey performed in organic chemistry, Rice claims that a good agreement exists between actual use figures and faculty judgment on which titles are important.

A somewhat different application of citation data can be found in a study by McCain and Bobick (1981). They used citations in faculty publications, doctoral dissertations, and preliminary doctoral qualifying briefs as a proxy for actual journal use figures in a departmental library. The assumption is that journals most cited by faculty and doctoral students are those most used and, more importantly, those least cited, or not cited at all, are those least used. The authors claim to have "identified a pool of less-productive journal titles which may be candidates for cancellation" but do not list these titles or indicate whether these appear to be "reasonable" candidates for cancellation according to other criteria. This procedure must be used with great caution because some periodicals (e.g., those read mostly for current news) may be heavily used but little if ever cited. Another factor to be considered is that certain titles may not be heavily used in a library because most library users have personal copies (Stenstrom and McBride, 1979). The more specialized the library, the more likely this is to be true.

In conclusion, while citation data may be of some value in identifying journals to acquire in some field—e.g., in establishing a new library—for reasons mentioned earlier they are less likely to be of much aid to deselection decisions.

Decisions Based on Multiple Factors

Wherever possible, it would seem desirable to base cancellation decisions on more than one criterion. In fact, the ideal situation might be one in which the librarian was able to give some numerical score to each periodical, the overall score being the sum of a number of component scores.

Suppose one decides that the criteria to be taken into consideration are: degree of use, opinion, cost, and the correlation between subject matter and institutional interests. Of these, only the cost figures are readily available. To gather the other needed data would require an in-house use study, a survey of user (e.g., faculty) opinion, and some form of subject classification applied to journals and to institutional interests (as in the collection/curriculum comparisons discussed in Chapter 3).

If all these data were collected, it would still be necessary to allocate a weight to each criterion and then to determine how many "points" a journal earns for each. With a maximum score of 100, one might allocate points as follows:

1. 50 for use
2. 20 for user opinion
3. 15 for relatedness
4. 15 for cost

For each criterion a scale of values, related to the allocated points, must be established, as in the following examples:

Uses per week

0-1	2-5		30+
0	5		50

Cost

$200+	180+		$0
0	1		15

A journal with 30 or more recorded uses per week gets the maximum score of 50, whereas one with no uses or one use scores no points, one with 2 to 5 uses scores 5, and so on. A journal costing $200 or more to subscribe to get no points on the cost scale while one costing the library nothing earns the maximum 15 points.

A similar point scale would be developed for the other evaluation criteria so that each journal in the collection would eventually receive a point total thereby allowing all titles to be ranked by numerical score. Even though use is given the lion's share of the score, one would probably apply a scoring system of this kind only to titles having some level of recorded use. Data from Pittsburgh and elsewhere (e.g., Holland, 1976) suggest that large academic libraries may receive substantial numbers of periodicals that are never used. Presumably these items would be the first to be considered in cancellation decisions.

This is all entirely hypothetical in terms of the criteria and scoring procedures; it is presented to illustrate how multiple criteria can be combined to arrive at a single score and should not be considered as a procedure advocated by the author.

This type of approach was described by Broude (1978) who combined no fewer than seven separate criteria into his "deselection model" as follows:

	Points allocated
1. Subscription cost	13
2. Average annual use	29
3. Impact factor	6
4. Number of indexing/abstracting services covering it	12
5. Availability in another local library	6
6. Reputation of publisher	4
7. Curriculum relatedness	30

For two of these criteria the point scale would be reversed, with the highest score for the lowest cost and the lowest level of local availability.

One problem with this approach lies in the allocation of points. Librarians may differ as to the relative weights to be assigned to the various criteria. The allocation proposed by Broude does seem "reasonable" in that it gives most weight to the local use factors (2 and 7).

A weighting procedure of the type described by Broude is certainly intriguing. If one could also devise a procedure for "estimating" scores for newly published journals, one could compare the projected scores with the actual scores of titles owned, thus facilitating decisions on selection as well as deselection. In a zero growth situation, a title in, say, agriculture might be added if its projected score greatly exceeds the scores of some titles already held. Depending on cost, a librarian might decide to add one title and cancel two others.

With Broude's model, however, only values for criteria 1 and (possibly) 6 would be known at the time a journal was first published, although values for the important criterion of 7 could be established on the basis of a detailed description of the journal's intended scope.

In point of fact, Broude's criteria are too numerous. Moreover, some appear redundant. For example, curriculum relatedness should correlate fairly closely with use. In fact, if it does not, it has little value as an evaluation criterion. If it is found to correlate closely with use, it can substitute for the use data.*

---

*A good predictor of use would have to take into account more factors than curriculum relatedness alone. For example, Holland (1976) found that foreign-language titles accounted for 10% of the periodicals budget but received only 1.5% of the use, while cover-to-cover translations consumed 22% of the budget but received only 1.6% of use. Popular news items and other periodicals not purchased in direct support of the curriculum would need to be treated differently.

From a cost-effectiveness point of view, the only salient criteria are 1 and 2. The journals that represent the best investment are those whose cost per use is at the low end of the scale. The cost considered can be cost of subscription only or cost of "ownership," including handling and storage costs. If curriculum relatedness correlates closely with use, a ranking based on cost per use may not differ too much from one based on all of Broude's criteria. Moreover, a numerical score for curriculum relatedness could substitute for actual use figures so the cost-effectiveness measure would relate the cost to this numerical score. The advantage of this simplification, of course, is that the score can be applied to newly published journals as well as existing ones, so that it could be used as a tool in selection as well as cancellation.

Flynn (1979) recommends that "expected cost per use" should be the criterion applied in periodical acquisition decisions. However, the only guidance he gives on how one should establish estimated use is that it be based on the "worth" of the journal. Curriculum relatedness* is a little more concrete.

A different approach to "scoring" a journal has been described by Johnson and Trueswell (1978). Journals may be ranked by a "criteria statistic score" which is merely the sum of the criteria that a particular title satisfies (a title that satisfies eight criteria gets a score of 8) or by a "weighted criteria statistic score" which takes into account the number of times a title satisfies each criterion. A title may satisfy any or all of these criteria: be recorded as photocopied in the library, be used often in the past year, be one that an individual claims to be of interest although he has not used it in the past year, be one in which library users have published in the past 5 years, be one that library users have cited in their publications, or be one citing the publications of library users. Apart from the first, all data are collected by means of a survey of users, which makes the whole process very cumbersome. It would only be viable in a relatively small research institution.

It has been assumed so far that the purpose of identifying a little used periodical is to discontinue it. An alternative strategy would be to improve cost per use by deliberately promoting the use of such items— displaying them prominently or advertising their existence in some other way.

---

*It is assumed that "curriculum relatedness" really refers to the extent to which the subject matter of the periodical matches institutional interests (research, teaching, or whatever). While this measure may be difficult to adapt to the public library environment, it should be as relevant to industrial and governmental libraries as it is to academic and research libraries.

This chapter has discussed the use of various types of data in making decisions on which periodicals should be discontinued and, to a lesser extent, which should be newly acquired. It was concluded that such decisions should be made primarily on the basis of cost-effectiveness. Cost-effectiveness aspects of the storage of periodicals are discussed in the next chapter. Some other cost-effectiveness aspects relating to collection development are dealt with in Chapter 13.

Study Questions

1. How many different ways of ranking periodicals on the basis of bibliometric data can you identify? Which rankings are likely to be most useful to a librarian in making deselection decisions?

2. Because of severe budget cuts, the University of Illinois Library (Urbana-Champaign) must reduce its expenditure on current periodical subscriptions by 15%. How would you determine which titles to discontinue? You must have hard facts to counter possible criticisms from the faculty.

3. Do you agree with the "point allocation" associated with Broude's deselection model? If not, what allocation would you propose and why? If you were asked to develop a new deselection model for an academic library what components would you include and how would you allocate points to them?

4. What components would you include in a deselection model for an industrial library and what would be your point allocation?

5. Stankus and Rice found that a ranking of periodicals by citation impact factor agreed closely with ranking by use figures (academic library) in some subject fields but not others. What are the possible explanations for this? How would you determine which explanation is most plausible?

6. You are the librarian of a large urban high school. Because of financial constraints, the periodical collection is in a "steady state" condition. To begin a subscription to a new periodical you must discontinue enough existing subscriptions to cover the cost of the new purchase. What data would you use to compare the value of the new title with the value of existing subscriptions? The library now subscribes to 150 titles.

6. Obsolescence, Weeding, and the Utilization of Space

The term "obsolescence," as applied to library materials, refers to the decline in use of these materials as they get older: the words "aging" and "decay" have been used as synonyms. Obsolescence is sometimes expressed as a "half life" (Burton and Kebler, 1960). The half life of an item is that period of time up to which it receives one half of all the uses it will receive. Putting this in a library context, consider the case of 10 books on various facets of biochemistry added to the collection in 1960. If circulation records for these items are available, one might find that they have collectively accounted for 180 uses by the end of 1986. But half of these circulations, 90, had occurred after their first six years in the library—say by the end of 1966—which puts their half life at about 6 years. Of course, this half life is not absolute because the books may be borrowed again in the future. Nevertheless, it will probably be a long time before enough further uses occur to change the half life, if in fact it ever is changed.

By drawing samples from portions of the collection (e.g., through use of the shelf list), and studying their circulation, one can determine the rate at which various subject fields are aging within the library. The data will usually be presented as graphs or tables, plotting decline in use over the years, although half life figures could also be used. A classic study of this type was performed at the University of Chicago, by Fussler and Simon (1969), who were able to confirm that the age of library materials is a good predictor of their use.

To draw collection samples and plot the use of these items over time can be a laborious process. Another possibility exists—taking current circulation and plotting, backwards in time, the publication dates of materials borrowed. Suppose, for example, that one takes all circulation records for agriculture items borrowed during, say, the month of April, 1987, and records the publication dates of the items borrowed. These can then be plotted as follows:

Year of publication	Number of items	
1987	25	
1986	115	
1985	172	*(cont.)*

72

Year of publication	Number of items
1984	81
1983	53
1982	29
1981	17
1980	8
Before 1980	85

The total number of items borrowed is 585, but about half of all items borrowed have been published within the last three years. The *median use age* is about 3 years. This is taken to be an estimate of obsolescence. The shorter the median use age the more rapidly a field is obsolescing.

In this method, one is estimating obsolescence by working from the present into the past whereas, in the collection sample method, one is doing the reverse. Line and Sandison (1974) refer to the former as *synchronous* obsolescence and to the latter as *diachronous*. A number of investigators have assumed that synchronous obsolescence is about the same as diachronous obsolescence—for example, that a median use age of 5 years equates with a half life of 5 years. Line and Sandison dispute this, claiming that there is no reason why synchronous obsolescence should be a good predictor of diachronous obsolescence, which they regard as the "true" measure. Based on citation rather than library use, Stinson and Lancaster (1987) produce evidence to suggest that obsolescence measured synchronously should be approximately the same as obsolescence measured diachronously.*

The librarian's interest in obsolescence is practical rather than theoretical. If use declines with age, one should be able to discard items on the basis of age or at least move older items to less accessible and less costly storage. This applies particularly to periodical titles. If one can show, for example, that 98% of the current use of a particular periodical is accounted for by volumes no more than 10 years old, it might make sense to move the earlier volumes to a less accessible location in the stacks or even into some form of remote storage.

Decline in use with age will be more rapid in some subject areas than in others, although one cannot generalize much about differences

---

*Obsolescence can be measured on the basis of citation as an alternative to library use. The half life of a periodical article is the time elapsing from date of publication to a point at which it has received one-half of all the citations it will ever receive. To measure obsolescence synchronously, one takes a sample of currently published articles in some field and records the publication dates of items cited in these. The *median citation age* is the period of time, from the present into the past, needed to account for one-half of all the citations made in the current literature.

among broad fields. The rate of obsolescence in the social sciences as a whole does not seem much different from that in the sciences as a whole (see, for example, Soper, 1972, and Van Styvendaele, 1981), but the humanities tend to have a much slower rate of obsolescence.* Some areas of the social sciences are undoubtedly aging more rapidly than some areas of the sciences. Even in the sciences, one field will age more rapidly than another, whether measured by citation or library use. Exhibit 15, for example, shows data for journal use gathered in six departmental libraries at the University of Pittsburgh (Kent et al., 1979). These data indicate that computer science and physics are aging most rapidly. Materials more than 10 years old are still being used at significant levels in chemistry, and materials more than 20 years old are still being used in mathematics. In a study of obsolescence in the literature of music, Griscom (1983) found marked differences between musicology (slow aging) and music education and theory (fairly rapid aging).

PERCENTAGE USE BY AGE

Age (years)	Physics	Life sciences	Engineering	Chemistry	Computer science	Mathematics
0-1	67.8	34.1	41.3	36.9	54.2	23.3
2-5	82.8	66.3	73.9	65.7	83.4	56.6
6-10	90.9	84.3	87.3	82.0	87.6	63.3
11-15	94.2	91.4	93.7	93.3	95.9	80.0
16-20	96.1	95.7	96.0	94.6	100	90.0
21-25	98.2	97.6	98.3	95.2	100	96.7
26+	100	100	100	100	100	100

Exhibit 15

Decline in use of periodicals with age in six departmental
libraries at the University of Pittsburgh. Reprinted from Kent et al.
(1979) by courtesy of Marcel Dekker Inc.

It is tempting for the librarian to think in terms of how far back one needs to hold periodicals to account for a specified percentage of total use. Strain (1966) refers to a *point of obsolescence*, defined as the date beyond which less than 15% of all current use occurs. Chen (1972) estimated this to be 14.5 years for physics materials used in the MIT

---

*Studies of obsolescence in the humanities are few and far between. Soper (1972) gives data for the humanities as a whole and Longyear (1977) and Griscom (1983) present results for the literature of music.

Science Library. However, Chen's data show that one cannot generalize about obsolescence even in a limited subject field: different periodicals have different aging characteristics.

To get a true picture of aging, other variables must be properly controlled. In particular, it is necessary to control for the amount of material available to be used. To give a concrete example, suppose data were collected on periodicals used in a medical library during some period in 1987. For 1986 issues, 500 uses are recorded while for 1981 issues only 250 uses occur. This seems a clear indication of decline in use with age. However, because of literature growth and other factors, the library may have on its shelves twice as much 1986 material as it has 1981 material. In this case, no evidence of obsolescence has been found: in relation to the 1986 material, the 1981 material is used exactly at the level that probability dictates. Relating use of materials to shelf space occupied can be referred to as "density of use." It can be considered the library use equivalent of the citation *impact factor*.

Sandison (1974) reworked the data published by Chen (1972) on the obsolescence of physics materials in the MIT Science Library, making allowances for the amount of space occupied by periodicals of various ages. Sandison discovered an "immediacy effect": the two most recent years were used more than probability would suggest they should be used. Beyond this two-year threshold, however, no evidence of obsolescence could be found: the materials were used at about the level expected based on amount of shelf space occupied.

Sandison's results are remarkably similar to the findings of Price (1980) on obsolescence as measured by citation. Price found this same immediacy effect: the most recent years are cited more frequently than they should be on the basis of probability, but earlier years are cited at the level expected when the amount of material published in various years is taken into account.

Quite different conclusions were arrived at by Sullivan et al. (1981). In a large academic medical library, they observed a regular decline in use with age whether or not a correction was made for shelf space occupied by periodicals of different ages.

Sandison (1981) is critical of Sullivan et al., perhaps because their results do not support his own, and points out that "use patterns for one journal or in one library can never be assumed to apply to another."

While conflicting evidence of this type exists, one can at least say that studies performed in libraries consistently show that materials with earlier publication dates tend to be used less than those with more recent publication dates, even if it is not yet proven conclusively that this is due to a true aging effect.

Weeding

Past use can be considered the criterion of most value in deciding which books to retire to less accessible storage or which to remove from the library completely. The last circulation date method, as described in Chapter 3, can be used to establish a retirement policy likely to have a negligible effect on the overall performance of the library. For example, if all books not circulating within the past eight years were retired, this might account for no more than 1% of current use but might allow retirement of 40% or more of the entire collection. Alternatively, the "dotting" method described in Chapter 4 would identify those monographs that have received no use within a particular period of time as well as indicating how far back each periodical has been used.

The age of books has been shown to be a good predictor of actual use and might substitute for use data in the retirement of materials by broad subject category, especially when used in conjunction with other criteria such as language (Fussler and Simon, 1969).

An effective weeding program can improve cost-effectiveness of the library by moving little used materials to less expensive storage areas. Nevertheless, there are costs associated with weeding itself: in identifying which materials to discard or relocate, in the alteration of catalog and shelf list records (to indicate new locations), and in retrieving materials from remote storage when requested by users. Different types of "costs" are those associated with user inconvenience, caused by delays in delivery of stored items, and possible loss of circulation due to items not being immediately available. Cost aspects of weeding are discussed by Raffel and Shishko (1969), Lister (1967), and Simon (1967), and cost aspects of storage alternatives by Ellsworth (1969) and Buckland et al. (1970), among others. The weeding of collections in libraries devoted to science and technology is discussed in Mount (1986).

McClellan (1956) has described a systematic approach to weeding the collection in a public library. When the need for the revision of a class has been established (on the basis of criteria mentioned in Chapter 3), all books published before a "period of depreciation" (10 years for science and technology, 15 years for the humanities, 5 years for fiction) are removed from the shelf for examination. Books in reasonable physical condition are returned to the shelf if they have circulated within the preceding two years or are judged to be of "standard value." Books in poor physical condition are replaced if they meet other criteria for retention. All other books withdrawn from the shelves are discarded or, in some cases, transferred to a "reserve stock."

Space Utilization

Weeding can improve the quality of a collection. When old and unused books are removed, the shelves appear more attractive to users and it is easier for them to find the newer or more popular items they are likely to be looking for. An effective weeding program has been known to increase circulation (Slote, 1982).

However, the main reason for weeding a collection is to save space or, more accurately, to optimize the use of space available to the library. A library may own space of varying degrees of accessibility to the public: open-access shelves, stacks, and off-site storage. From a cost-effectiveness point of view, occupancy of this space should be related to the anticipated use of materials. In particular, the materials stored on open shelves should be those likely to achieve most use relative to the space consumed.

Take, as one example, an industrial library having space to store 3000 bound volumes of 200 periodical titles on open access shelves. Assuming an average of two volumes per year per periodical, all titles could be held for 7 years back (200 x 2 x 7 = 2800 volumes). This is unlikely to be an efficient strategy. Some titles may still be used at a reasonable level when they are 10 or more years old while others may hardly be used at all after 5 years, and a few may be virtually dead after 2 or 3 years. To use the space efficiently, density of use (e.g., use per meter of shelving occupied) must be taken into account (Brookes, 1970). This has been clearly stated by Line (1977):

> Data on the age of journals cited are of no value for discarding purposes unless they are related to the physical shelf occupancy of volumes of different ages. A volume of 1950 2cm thick which receives 20 uses is earning its keep as much as a volume of 1975 4cm thick which receives 40 uses. (Page 429)

Groos (1969) was able to show how limited space for storage of periodicals could be optimized by considering alternative strategies in which the number of titles and the number of years held are varied. His results are summarized in Exhibit 16. The number of requests satisfied in the period considered was 1172. All 57 periodical titles need to be held as far back as they go to satisfy all requests. But more than half of all requests would be satisfied if these 57 titles were held only 6 to 7 years back. The three most productive titles alone would satisfy 48% of requests if held back to 1900. The first six titles held back to 1900 would satisfy 68% of requests and the first ten titles held back to 1946 would satisfy 69%. In terms of space utilization, the optimum strategy might be to hold the first 17 titles back to the beginning; this would satisfy 90% of requests.

Number and percentage of periodical article requests satisfied related to number of titles and years held				
Years held	Titles 1-3	Titles 1-6	Titles 1-10	Titles 1-17	Titles 1-57
1960-1966	269 (23%)	444 (38%)	501 (43%)	556 (47%)	621 (53%)
1946-1966	474 (40%)	716 (61%)	809 (69%)	898 (77%)	996 (85%)
1900-1966	559 (48%)	801 (68%)	923 (79%)	1035 (88%)	1150 (98%)
0-1966	561 (48%)	803 (69%)	941 (80%)	1053 (90%)	1172 (100%)

Exhibit 16

Use of shelf space related to number of periodical titles held
and number of years held. Adapted from Groos (1969) by permission of Aslib

Taylor (1977) developed a "consultation factor" to account for use of shelf space. This consultation factor is defined as number of consultations per day per 1000 meters of shelving occupied: $C_i = \dfrac{1000 \times n_i}{d \times L_i}$

where n_i = number of consultations
   L_i = length of shelves
   d = number of days of survey.

The consultation factor is a numerical value that increases when the number of uses increases or the shelf space occupied decreases. For example, the same numerical value of 10 is derived from

$$\frac{1000 \times 11}{22 \times 50} \quad \text{and} \quad \frac{1000 \times 22}{22 \times 100}$$

In the former, a title occupying 50 meters of space receives 11 uses over the 22-day survey period. In the latter, a title occupying 100 meters of space receives 22 uses, an average of 1 a day during the period of the survey.

The effect of ranking journals by density of use instead of "raw use" is shown in Exhibit 17. Title A receives twice the use that title G receives but occupies six times the amount of space. Title G is the highest ranked journal on the basis of density of use. The journals can be ranked, according to the two criteria, as follows:

Raw use	Density of use
B	G
A	B
C, F	F, H
E	E
G	C
D	A
H	D

The top six journals in the raw use ranking account for 86% of the use but occupy 18 units of shelf space whereas the top six in the use density ranking account for 84% of the use, yet occupy only 13 units of space. Good examples of the practical application of density of use data can be found in the work of Mankin and Bastille (1981) and Wenger and Childress (1977). The latter carry the process further by developing a "balance index" for each subject area represented in the periodical collection. The index is obtained by dividing the subject's use per shelf space figure by the average for the collection as a whole. An index of 1.0 is said to indicate an ideal balance, a value greater than 1.0 is said to indicate that more titles should be added, while a value of less than 1.0 might indicate that some titles should be candidates for cancellation.

Title	Units of space occupied	Number of uses	Density of use (uses per unit of space)
A	☐ ☐ ☐ ☐ ☐ ☐	18	18/6 = 3.0
B	☐ ☐ ☐ ☐	25	25/4 = 6.2
C	☐ ☐ ☐	12	12/3 = 4.0
D	☐ ☐ ☐	8	8/3 = 2.7
E	☐ ☐	10	10/2 = 5.0
F	☐ ☐	12	12/2 = 6.0
G	☐	9	9/1 = 9.0
H	☐	6	6/1 = 6.0

Exhibit 17
Hypothetical raw use and density of use
data for eight periodicals

In some libraries retention periods for periodicals have been established on the basis of user opinion—e.g., through consultation with faculty members (Schloman and Ahl, 1979)—rather than from use or use-density data. This procedure may be acceptable if it can be shown that this would lead to decisions very similar to those made on more objective principles—perhaps rather unlikely.

When periodicals, or parts of periodicals, are removed from primary to secondary storage (e.g., some type of warehouse), such a move need not be considered permanent. A librarian should maintain records on frequency of use of stored titles, and how far back each is used. If the use of a title exceeds some expected value after several months in storage, the title would become a candidate for return to prime storage, possibly at the expense of some other title (Snowball and Sampedro, 1973).

Effect of Location on Use

Mueller (1965), Harris (1966), and Pings (1967), among others, have shown that a librarian can influence patterns of use by changing the physical accessibility of various parts of the collection. In particular, the highlighting of certain books, by placing them on special displays, has been found to be rather effective as a means of promoting their use (Goldhor, 1972, 1981a). One suspects, in fact, that a colorful display on "Books that have never been borrowed" might be a great success.

Baker (1985) has tried to determine whether displays increase use because of the increased accessibility and visibility of books placed in prime locations or because the displays narrow the choice of readers by guiding them to a smaller selection of titles. Pretest-posttest experiments were performed at two small public libraries and users borrowing books were interviewed. The results suggest that the primary factor affecting use was accessibility. Selectivity was a lesser factor and seemed only to affect the larger of the two libraries.

Study Questions

1. Is there an "optimum" size for a book display in a public library? How would you determine what the optimum size is?

2. Using citation data, Stinson and Lancaster (1987) have produced some evidence to suggest that the rate of obsolescence of materials measured synchronously is equivalent to the rate of obsolescence measured diachronously. How would you compare synchronous and diachronous measures of obsolescence using library circulation data?

3. Sandison (1974) has presented data on decline in use of library materials with age that appear to be at odds with later data collected by Sullivan et al. (1981). Examine the two sets of data. Is there any logical explanation for the discrepancy in these results?

4. A small industrial library subscribes to 250 periodicals but has space to keep only 300 bound volumes of periodicals on open shelves. What data would you collect in order to decide how best to use this space? How would you collect the data?

7. Catalog Use

Chapters 2-6 have dealt almost exclusively with the first step of the chain of events depicted in Exhibit 2, that is with the question "Is the item owned?" Given that an item sought by a user is owned, it must still be found on the shelves of the library. This will frequently mean that the user must locate an entry for the item in the catalog of the library in order to determine its shelf location. This chapter deals with the next probability implied in the sequence of Exhibit 2, the probability that a user will find an entry in the catalog for an item sought.

"Catalog use studies" can be divided into two major categories:

1. Those studies designed to determine what proportion of the patrons of the library make use of the catalog. Studies of this kind may also try to distinguish between the characteristics of catalog users and those of nonusers, to determine how the catalog is used and for what purpose, and perhaps to discover why some library users never consult the catalog. A major study of this kind, involving many libraries in the United Kingdom, is described by Maltby (1971, 1973).
2. Those studies that focus on people known to use the catalog, the objective being to discover how they use it, for what purpose, and with what degree of success. Important studies of this kind have been performed by the American Library Association (1958), Lipetz (1970), and Tagliacozzo and Kochen (1970).

The first type of study will involve the use of questionnaires or interviews administered to random samples of library users. If information is needed on the behavior of catalog users, a *critical incident technique* is recommended. In this technique, the interview or questionnaire asks the respondent to focus on a particular use of the catalog rather than asking about his or her use of the catalog in general. The justification for this is that a person may be able to give fairly precise information on a single "critical" incident but might have considerable trouble in coming up with anything meaningful about his general behavior. The critical incident will usually be the latest incident.

If the critical incident technique is applied, the first question might well be something like "Can you remember when it was that you last used the catalog of this library?" If the respondent does remember, he is asked to concentrate on that incident and to reconstruct the event in as much detail as possible: what he was looking for, how he approached the search, and how successful he was.

The majority of "catalog use studies," however, are of the second type noted above; that is, they focus on people who are observed to be using the catalog. With an online catalog, it is possible to gather certain data on patterns of use unobtrusively—i.e., without the users knowing that their actions are recorded or observed. In general, however, one can only get useful details about how a person consults a catalog by asking him. Printed questionnaires could be employed for this purpose but interviews are likely to produce much better results. The interviewer will follow a particular "schedule" of questions.

Interviews could be conducted with a catalog user:

1. When he is observed to leave the catalog having, presumably, completed a search.
2. When he is observed to approach the catalog, before conducting a search.
3. Before and after use of the catalog.
4. Throughout use of the catalog.

Superficially, the first of these options seems most desirable. Since the subject will not know that he will later be interviewed, the data gathering process can have no influence on his behavior. If all one wants to know is whether or not the user found one or more "useful" entries, it might be sufficient to perform a post-search interview. On the other hand, for more accurate information on the success rate in catalog use, and on factors affecting this success, one will probably need to interview the user before the search begins. Of course, this may introduce some "Hawthorne effect": a user who knows he is being observed might behave a little differently than he would otherwise.

Nevertheless, a slight Hawthorne effect may be preferable to having post-search information without having corresponding pre-search information. It is important to know what a user thinks he is looking for before he consults the catalog. It is also important to know what information he brings to the search and how complete and accurate this information is (e.g., does he have title but no author, surname only, initials but not full forenames, is title correct, is author name correct?).

A catalog user will be influenced by what he finds or fails to find while performing a search. After the search, what he claims to have been looking for may not be identical with what he would have claimed to be seeking before the process began. This is most likely in the case of a subject search (e.g., before—books on athletics; after—books on the Olympic Games) but an author/title search might also be affected. For example, in a post-search interview someone might claim to have been looking for a book called *The Information Machines* by Bagdikian.

Before the search, he might have said he was looking for a book by Bagdikian on the future of the newspaper industry.

After a search, too, it may be difficult to find out accurately what information the user brought with him to the catalog: he may have forgotten that he only had initials and not full forenames or that the spelling of a name in the catalog was somewhat different from the spelling he expected.

Of course, it is of little use interviewing a user before a catalog search if he is not also interviewed afterwards. Despite the Hawthorne effect, one is likely to get the most complete information on catalog use by interviewing a random sample of users before they search the catalog and again later. Before the search, the interviewer determines what the user is looking for, how he intends to proceed, and what information he has. After the search, the interviewer tries to get the user to reconstruct what he did at the catalog and to determine how successful the process has been. Some supplementary information might be obtained by observing the user from a distance—e.g., which part of the catalog he goes to first, how many drawers he consults, and so on.

Studies have been performed in which the interviewer accompanies the library user throughout the search. While this is the most obtrusive of techniques, it can produce data that would be difficult to collect in any other way. For example, the user can be asked to explain why he approached the search in a particular way and the interviewer is able to record the entire sequence of events that takes place. This is particularly important in the case of a subject search where it might be valuable to know which heading is consulted first, whether the user follows up on cross-references, whether the user finds entries that suggest books relevant to his interests, and so on. The "running interview" can be valuable if it is conducted with great skill. The interviewer must be very careful to avoid influencing the searcher's behavior by helping him in any way and this is sometimes very difficult to do.

One of the most elaborate (and obtrusive) of catalog use studies was performed by Markey (1983) in one university, three public, four college, and four high school libraries in Ohio. Tape recorders were used to record the spoken thoughts ("protocols") of individuals as they performed subject searches. Where necessary, the investigator prompted the searcher to verbalize. For each search it was possible to collect details concerning the user, a statement of the search topic and the purpose of the search, the information brought to the search by the user, the tape recording of "spoken thoughts," and the interviewer's observations on the searcher's behavior.

Some studies of catalog use have been conducted within a single institution through questionnaires mailed to a sample of library users. One recent investigation of this kind was performed at the Australian National University (Wood, 1984).

Whichever method is used, it will be necessary for the evaluator to arrive at some acceptable procedure for selecting users at random for inclusion in the study. This will usually be accomplished by selecting random time slots in days that have also been selected at random. Lipetz (1970) gives excellent guidance on sampling for a large scale catalog use study.

The great majority of catalog searches will be performed either to:

1. Determine whether or not the library owns a particular book or other item—*known item search*. The user will presumably have details on author or title or both, or
2. Identify items owned by the library that deal with a particular subject—*subject search*.

Known Item Search

This type of search is much easier to deal with than the subject search. A known item search is successful if the user locates an entry for the item sought and unsuccessful if he fails to locate such an entry. For evaluation purposes, however, one needs to be able to distinguish collection failures from catalog use failures—i.e., differentiate the case in which a user fails to find an entry actually present in the catalog from the case in which he fails to find an entry because the item is not owned. For each known item search that results in failure, then, the search must be repeated carefully by one or more experienced librarians to see if the user overlooked an entry present in the catalog.

Results from previous studies suggest that the success rate for known item searches in the card catalogs of large academic libraries may be about 80% on the average. That is, the user fails to find an entry actually present for about one search in every five. This success rate is likely to vary from one library to another depending on size—the larger the library, the larger and more complex the catalog—and on characteristics of the catalog itself. It is also likely to vary with type of user. The results for online catalogs could well be better on the average than those for card catalogs, but not enough comparative data exist to prove this point.*

---

*Jones (1986) and Dickson (1984) present results that suggest that the failure rate for author/title searches in online catalogs may fall in the range of 10-20%.

An important element in a catalog use study will be an analysis of the reasons why users fail to find entries present in the catalog. The results of previous studies suggest that the following factors are all important:

1. The user's previous experience with library catalogs and with the one now being studied in particular.
2. The user's general intelligence and perseverance.
3. The amount and quality of information brought by the user to the catalog. For example, does he have complete and correct author information and/or complete and correct title information? It has been found that, in general, a user is more likely to have accurate information on the title of a book than he is to have complete and accurate information on the name of the author.
4. The search approach followed by the user. Most users will search under names of authors despite the fact that their title information may well be somewhat better.
5. The number of access points provided by the catalog—e.g., the extent to which title entries are included and the extent to which cross-references occur.
6. Whether the catalog is a dictionary catalog or one that is split and, if so, how it is split.
7. Other characteristics of the catalog, including the extent of misfiling and the quality of the guiding or labeling.

Subject Searches

In the case of a known item search, the user either finds what he is looking for or he does not. This simple binary situation does not apply to a subject search. One cannot say that such a search has or has not been successful in any absolute sense. Instead, one must be concerned with *how successful* it has been.

The evaluation of subject searches is much more difficult than the evaluation of known item searches, which explains why much better data exist on the latter situation than on the former. The main problem faced by the evaluator is to arrive at some useful measure of "success" for a subject search. In the past, many investigators have adopted criteria that are far from perfect. At the crudest level, a search is judged successful if the user is able to match his search terms with those used in the catalog. Thus, if he looks for books on higher education and finds the subject heading HIGHER EDUCATION in the catalog, the search is considered a success.* Other investigators have judged a search to be successful if, as a result, the user selects one or more books as being of possible use to him.

This latter criterion is certainly much better than the simple "matching" criterion. Nevertheless, it is not adequate. One really wants to know to what extent the items found by the user satisfy his needs and whether or not he overlooked other items that would be judged more useful than the ones actually discovered. For certain types of searches one would also be concerned with completeness—did the user find all the books owned by the library on the subject? Finally, some measure of user effort is desirable: how long did it take to satisfy an information need or how long did it take to find how many useful items?

In point of fact, the evaluation of a subject search in the catalog of a library is not significantly different from the evaluation of a subject search in any other type of bibliographic data base in printed or electronic form. The evaluation of subject searches in bibliographic data bases is dealt with in Chapter 11.

Simulations

Some types of research studies relating to catalog use have been performed through simulations. One form of simulation involves the use of students or other individuals in some controlled task situation. For example, the students are asked to locate an entry for a particular title (see Gouke and Pease, 1982, for one study of this type) or to find books dealing with a particular subject. In a simpler kind of study, the subjects are asked to indicate which terms they would use to find information on some topic; these terms are then matched against the subject headings in the catalog in order to estimate the probability that a search would be successful. Useful information can be obtained in studies of this type if they are carefully conducted. The University of Chicago study of requirements for future catalogs (University of Chicago, 1968) is a notable example of a major study based largely on various simulations.

Online Catalogs

In principle, a study of the use made of an online catalog may not differ significantly from a study of the use of a catalog in card form. To

---

*In some studies a score is given to a search to reflect the degree of coincidence between the user's terms and the catalog's terms.

get complete information, including identification of the user and an unequivocal indication of whether or not a search is successful, interviews must be conducted with a sample of users (see Specht, 1980, for an example). Nevertheless, certain aggregate data can be collected through online monitoring, including data on volume of catalog use, use by day and time of day, use of terminals in various locations, and other data reflecting patterns of use: type of search performed, commands used, time expended, subject headings used, and so on.

It is also possible to record and print out, for subsequent study, a sample of the interactions that occur between the user and the system, or even to observe a user's search by means of a monitoring terminal. In this way, valuable information on user behavior and search strategy can be collected in an unobtrusive way. The monitoring of a user's search without that user's permission, even if anonymity is maintained, does raise ethical issues that suggest that these techniques must be used with some caution.

Certain types of simulations can also be applied to the online catalog situation. In particular, the use of problem-solving tasks is entirely appropriate in studies of how online catalogs are used and with what degree of success (an example can be found in Gouke and Pease, 1982).

In 1981 the Council on Library Resources funded five organizations to conduct a comprehensive study of user responses to public online catalogs. The participating organizations were the Library of Congress, the Research Libraries Group, the Online Computer Library Center, the University of California, and J. Matthews and Associates. The study involved thirty libraries of various kinds and seventeen different online systems. Questionnaires were completed at the terminal by over 8,000 catalog users as well as almost 4,000 nonusers of online catalogs. The study also included group interviews and the analysis of "transaction logs" (i.e., machine records of interactions between the users and the systems). The transaction logs gave details on the commands used, the sequence of actions, errors encountered, the time spent in a search, and the types of searches performed. Summaries of this important study can be found in Ferguson et al. (1982) and Kaske and Sanders (1983).

Lipetz and Paulson (1987) studied the impact of the introduction of an online subject catalog at the New York State Library. Their work confirms the observations of Markey (1984) that the introduction of online subject searching capabilities increases the proportion of subject searches performed by library users as well as leading to an overall increase in catalog use. They also gathered data suggesting that subject searches in online catalogs may be less successful than those in other forms of catalog—at least, users of the online catalog tend to feel less certain that their searches have been successful.

A useful summary and interpretation of research on online catalogs can be found in the work of Lewis (1987).

Chapters 2-7 have discussed evaluation procedures associated with the probability that a library will own an item sought by a user and that the user will be able to confirm this ownership. The probability that a user will be able to find an item owned is dealt with in Chapters 8 and 9.

Study Questions

1. A public library serving a population of 500,000 is planning to close its card catalogs and go entirely online. The online system is to be designed by an outside contractor according to technical specifications prepared by the library staff. Before the technical specifications can be prepared, it is necessary to learn more on how the present card catalogs are used, with what degree of success, and what problems users now have with the catalogs. How would you study use of the present catalogs to gather data valuable in preparing the technical specifications for the online catalog?

2. "An online catalog is merely a card catalog accessible electronically." Do you agree or disagree? Would it be possible to design an online catalog based on quite "unconventional" search approaches? Would it be useful to do so? What unconventional approaches might be used?

3. An online catalog has been in use in a small liberal arts college for a period of about two years. It has been observed that more subject searches are performed in the online catalog than was true for the card catalog it replaced. The director of the library wants to know how successful these subject searches are. Do users find materials that satisfy their needs? Do they find the "best" materials? How would you design a study to answer these?

8. Shelf Availability

The last steps of the chain in Figure 2 have to do with the probability that a user will find a book on the shelves of the library given that he has located an entry for it in the catalog. A shelf availability study can be performed through simulation or it can be achieved by a survey of library users. A review of availability studies has recently been completed by Mansbridge (1986).

Simulation

Suppose one could compile a list of, say, 300 references representing bibliographic items typical of those that users of a particular library would likely be seeking. An investigator could enter the library on a selected day to see how many of these items are owned by the library and how many of the owned items are immediately available. Let us say that 212 of the items are located in the catalog and that 174 of these are found by the investigator on the shelves of the library. Three probabilities have been established (De Prospo et al., 1973):

1) The probability of ownership, which was found to be 212/300 or approximately .7.
2) The probability of availability for an item owned: 174/212 or .82.
3) The probability that the item will be both owned and available, which is the product of the two component probabilities, namely .7 x .82, or .57.

Based on a sample of 300 bibliographic references, then, the investigator has shown that a user of the library faces about a 70% chance that an item looked for will be owned, an 82% chance that an owned item will be immediately available on the shelves, and a 57% chance that an item sought will be both owned and available.

The study described can be considered to simulate a situation in which 300 users walk into the library on a particular day, each one seeking a single bibliographic item. The results indicate that 57 out of each 100 users can leave the library with the sought item in hand.

In performing such a study, one will want to do more than arrive at these probabilities, important though they are, and conduct an analysis to determine the whereabouts of the books that were unavailable on the shelves. Possible sources of "failure" will include:

1. Item on loan to another user.
2. Item in use in the library.
3. Item waiting to be reshelved.

4. Item misplaced on the shelf.
5. Item away at a bindery.
6. Item unaccounted for.

Through such an analysis, the investigator identifies all of the factors affecting the probability of availability of an item owned. For one thing, the study shows to what extent a user may be frustrated by "interference" from other users (Saracevic et al., 1977). A library functions as a kind of competitive environment in which the users compete with each other for the library's resources. As suggested in Chapter 3, because of the way that demand is distributed, most users are competing for essentially the same small group of materials.

The analysis of causes of failure may also reveal some sources of internal inefficiency. Perhaps misshelving is found to be a serious problem, or significant numbers of failures may be due to unacceptable delays in reshelving books after they are returned from circulation, or an unexpectedly large number of books cannot be accounted for, suggesting the need for more stringent security measures.

A simulation of the type described can give a very reliable estimate of shelf availability, providing that the sample of bibliographic items used can be shown to be truly representative of the document needs of the users of the library. This is relatively easy to achieve for a specialized or scholarly library but rather difficult in the case of a general or popular one.

Let us consider a study of shelf availability in an academic medical library. It seems reasonable to assume that the types of journal articles that will be looked for in the library are those appearing in *Index Medicus*, and the types of monographs are those appearing in the *Current Catalog* of the National Library of Medicine. Thus, one could use the latest issues of these two bibliographies as the source from which to draw random samples of items for a study of ownership and availability. Alternatively, one could take *Index Medicus* as a source for an initial sample and use the bibliographic references in these items as a "pool" from which a final sample is drawn.

The procedure might work as follows. Suppose 300 references are drawn at random from the latest monthly issue of *Index Medicus*. All of these journal articles are obtained (where necessary, through interlibrary loan) and their bibliographies copied. If each article contains 12 references on the average, a pool of 3600 bibliographic references has been formed. From this pool, 300* can be drawn at random to use as the sample for the availability study.

---

*As reported by Orr et al. (1968a), with a sample of 300, one can be 95% confident that the results from repeated testing, with other samples of the same size and drawn in a similar way, will not vary from the original results by more than 5% in either direction.

This procedure is more laborious and complicated than simply drawing the final sample directly from *Index Medicus,* but it has certain advantages: it represents items of varying ages (whereas the direct sample represents only the more recent materials) and it reflects various types of documents—articles, monographs, reports, government publications—in proportion to the way in which these items are cited in the journal literature of medicine. Because monographs tend not to be heavily cited, however, this type of sample may well underrepresent demand for monographic materials in an academic medical library. By using indexing and abstracting services in this way, it should be possible to arrive at "availability samples" that realistically reflect the document needs of users of any type of special library.

Arriving at an acceptable sample for the evaluation of ownership and availability in a public library is a much more difficult proposition. DeProspo et al. (1973) used three samples in their work in public libraries:

1. A sample of 500 books selected at random from recent years of the *American Book Publishing Record* (ABPR).
2. A sample of 80 bibliographic references drawn from periodical indexes commonly held in public libraries. Later (Altman et al., 1976) this sample was changed to one consisting of 40 *journal titles* drawn from each of eight indexes commonly held in public libraries (*Applied Science and Technology Index, Art Index, Biological and Agricultural Index, Business Periodicals Index, Education Index, Public Affairs Information Service, Readers' Guide,* and *Social Sciences Index*).
3. A sample of 500 items drawn at random from the shelf list of the library.

The second of these can be considered a completely separate sample used to determine both ownership and availability of periodical articles in public libraries. It is a good sample in that it is likely to represent the types of periodical articles that users will seek in a public library.

As pointed out clearly by Bommer (1974), the other two samples have great problems associated with them. The ABPR sample is nothing more than one drawn at random from a list of everything available through normal publishing channels in North America. It is not a sample that is in any way "biased" toward the public library environment and is likely to contain a rather significant number of items of an esoteric nature that will appear in few if any public libraries. A sample of this kind, drawn from everything available, measures the size of the collection of a public library but tells us absolutely nothing about appropriateness to local needs. More importantly, since the standard used in the evaluation is drawn by random sampling, a public library would perform as well by buying books at random as it would through careful selection procedures.

This can be illustrated by considering three possible selection procedures adopted by three different public libraries:

A picks 500 books at random from the ABPR.

B selects 500 books from the ABPR that seem best to reflect the demands of the users of the library.

C picks 1,000 books at random from the ABPR.

When these three libraries are evaluated on the basis of 500 titles selected *at random* from the ABPR, probability dictates that library *A* will own about as many as library *B*, but *C* will own twice as many as either *B* or *A*. The test measures nothing more than size.

When this sample is applied to a very small public library, the number of items owned is likely to be so small that it would have no significance if used to estimate availability. It was for this reason that the shelf list sample was developed. The ABPR sample estimates ownership and the shelf list sample estimates availability. Thus, a small public library might score 31/500 on ownership and 425/500 on availability.

It should be recognized, however, that the ABPR sample could still have value in the evaluation of a library network or system, allowing estimates to be made of overall coverage as well as overlap and gaps (Clark, 1976).

At first sight, the shelf list sample appears to be perfectly valid. In fact, however, a shelf list sample used in a study of availability significantly biases the results in favor of the library. As discussed in Chapter 3, use is likely to be concentrated on a very small part of the collection. Most of the books will be very little used. Exhibit 18 shows a hypothetical collection divided into three levels of demand. In actual fact, most of the use comes from that third of the collection identified as "demand level 1." The items in level 3 are almost never used. But a random sample of 300, drawn from the shelf list, will include as many low demand items as high demand items. When the sample is applied to the library, actual availability levels will be greatly overestimated.

In real life, the chance that a user walking into this library will find a sought item available will be little more than .4. The shelf list sample, on the other hand, estimates availability at .66 $[(40/100 + 70/100 + 90/100)/3]$.

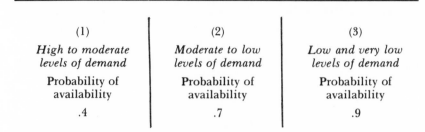

(1)	(2)	(3)
High to moderate levels of demand	*Moderate to low levels of demand*	*Low and very low levels of demand*
Probability of availability	Probability of availability	Probability of availability
.4	.7	.9

Exhibit 18
Library collection partitioned into three levels of demand

In actual fact, the results of an availability study based on a shelf list sample can be adjusted mathematically to eliminate this type of bias (Kantor, 1981 and Schwarz, 1983). On the other hand, there is a much better way of arriving at the sample in the first place, namely to draw it from the circulation records of the library.*

Suppose one drew a random sample of 500 items from all those recorded as out on loan on a particular day in April. This sample could then be applied to measure availability on a selected day in, say, October. Such a sample is superior to the shelf list sample in that its composition should correspond to the various levels of demand reflected in Exhibit 18. That is, most of the items will be Level 1 but there will also be some Level 2 items and a few Level 3 items, this distribution reflecting the actual distribution of demand over the collection as a whole.

The circulation sample, as described, solves the problem of estimating shelf availability in a public library but not the problem of estimating ownership. Drawing samples at random from bibliographic tools designed for the public library environment (e.g., the *Public Library Catalog* or the *Fiction Catalog*) is probably better than drawing from the ABPR, but carries its own dangers: if a public library uses the *Fiction Catalog* as its only source in the selection of fiction, that source is of little use as an evaluation tool for that library.

One way to arrive at a sample for estimating ownership in a public library is to draw it from items added to another public library in a similar type of community. Consider Library *A*, serving a population of 30,000 in a predominantly agricultural community. About 50 miles

---

*For this idea I am indebted to Kay Flowers, Head of Circulation and Systems, Fondren Library, Rice University, Houston, Texas.

away exists Library *B*, serving a predominantly agricultural community of about 100,000. A sample drawn at random from the "new book list" of *B*, assuming that such a publication is available, might be a useful sample to use for estimating ownership in Library *A*. Of course, it is better to use the larger library in the evaluation of the smaller than it is to use the smaller to evaluate the larger.

In the evaluation of document delivery, the general academic (e.g., undergraduate) library exhibits some of the same problems presented by the public library, although course reading lists might be used as a suitable source from which to draw samples. Wainwright and Dean (1976), for example, have described how undergraduate course reading lists were used in evaluation in colleges of advanced education in Australia. Items cited in texts required for various courses should be the kinds of things that students might well be looking for in the library.

Scoring Methods

In evaluating the performance of a single library, the derivation of scores reflecting simple probabilities seems most useful. In the *comparison* of libraries, however, alternative scoring procedures are possible.

In the "document delivery test," as developed by Orr et al. (1968a), the performance of a library was expressed as a *capability index* (CI), a value between 0 and 100 that reflects the speed with which the library can deliver items to users. As used by Orr, the CI was derived from a five-point scale expressing "estimated delivery time," as follows:

1. Item delivered to user in less than 10 minutes.
2. Delivery time is 10 minutes to 2 hours.
3. Delivery time is 2 hours to one day.
4. Delivery time is one day to one week.
5. Delivery time is over a week.

The forms used to collect data in the availability study can be printed to indicate all possible outcomes for a search. Each of these outcomes is pre-coded with a number to indicate estimated delivery time. For example, a book immediately available on open shelves would be coded 1, the best possible case, while an item that had to be delivered to the user from controlled access stacks might be coded 2 and an item away at a bindery could be coded 5. In this scoring procedure, no binary distinction is made between items owned and items not owned. If it is thought that a non-owned item could be acquired in less than a week (e.g., through interlibrary loan), it could be coded 4; if an interlibrary loan is likely to take more than a week it would be coded 5.

With a sample of 300 items, the scoring might be as follows:

70 items score 1   1 x 70 = 70
62 items score 2   2 x 62 = 124
44 items score 3   3 x 44 = 132
29 items score 4   4 x 29 = 116
95 items score 5   5 x 95 = 475

The *mean speed* derived from these results is 3 (917/300) approximately.
The equation for deriving the capability index is:

$$\frac{5 \text{ minus mean speed}}{4} \times 100$$

which, in this hypothetical case, would be

$$\frac{5 - 3}{4} \times 100, \text{ or } 50$$

Note that a library would have a CI of 100 if all items in the sample were
available in 10 minutes or less and a CI of zero if no item was available in
less than a week. Thus scored, the document delivery test is very discriminating in ranking libraries on their ability to deliver documents to
users expeditiously (Orr and Schless, 1972).

In a study of the availabilty of books in Illinois public libraries,
Wallace (1983) also used a scoring procedure that takes delivery speed
into account. A library can earn up to 10 points for a single book
appearing in the test. It receives all 10 points if the book is immediately
available. If this ideal situation does not apply, points are deducted
according to the following schedule:

Library offers to place reserve or obtain an interlibrary loan
    Book obtained in 1-3 days   Deduct 1
    Book obtained in 4-10 days   Deduct 2
    Book obtained in 11-17 days   Deduct 3
    Book obtained in 18-24 days   Deduct 4
    Book obtained in 25-31 days   Deduct 5
    Book obtained in 32-38 days   Deduct 6
    Book obtained in 39-45 days   Deduct 7
    Book obtained in 46-52 days   Deduct 8
    Book obtained in 53-59 days   Deduct 9
    Book obtained in 60 days or   Deduct 10
        more

If members of the library staff made no attempt to reserve an owned book
or obtain an unowned book on interlibrary loan, the library was given a
score of zero.

Wallace's study involved the use of "surrogate users." Each volunteer enters a library looking for one preselected title and records the actual outcome of this particular search.

Besides those already mentioned, simulation studies of document availability have been reported by Penner (1972), Ramsden (1978), and Murfin (1980).

User Surveys

As an alternative to the simulation method, a study of availability can be conducted through a type of user survey. One approach is simply to get users to record details of items they look for but are unable to find. This can be achieved by handing users brief questionnaires as they enter the library on those days chosen for the survey. Additional questionnaires can be made available at the catalog and other strategic points, and signs can be used to request the cooperation of users.

The survey can be designed to focus on shelf availability alone or on virtually all sources of failure. The form (it could be brief enough to fit on a small card) can be so designed that the user records: (a) details of items he is unable to find in the catalog, and (b) the fact that he was unable to find on the shelf an item for which he had found an entry in the catalog. On the other hand, the form could be designed only to record nonavailability on the shelf of an item for which the call number is known. In the first case, obviously, it would be possible to break down the failures into collection failures, catalog use failures, and shelf availability failures. In the latter case, only shelf availability is being studied.

Users are asked to return the completed failure form to a desk at the exit, to drop it into some form of collecting box, or (in some studies) to put it on the shelf where the book is supposed to be. In this type of study, the investigator must follow up immediately to determine the reasons for nonavailability of items (as discussed earlier in the chapter).

As described, this type of survey seeks the voluntary cooperation of all users who encounter failures to find sought items. If continued for a significant period of time, reliable data can be obtained on the relative impact of various sources of failure, but no absolute value for the number of failures occurring is achieved since not everyone encountering a failure will cooperate. Moreover, the method will not give a true *failure rate* because one will not know how many successes occur for each failure recorded. The number of items borrowed on the days of the survey gives some indication of "success" but the ratio of items borrowed to recorded failures will give a very imperfect picture of failure rate.

As with many other types of study, it is usually better to focus on a random sample of users, making a strong effort to secure their cooperation, rather than trying to achieve voluntary cooperation from everyone. In this case, every nth user entering the library is given a form by the investigator. The cooperation of the sampled users is requested and each is asked to return his form to the investigator as he leaves the library. As an alternative, the users could be contacted as they are seen to approach the catalog.

When focusing on a random sample of users in this way, interviews can replace the questionnaires. Each selected user is interviewed as he enters the library, to find out what he is looking for, and re-interviewed as he leaves to determine whether or not he was successful. In some studies (e.g., Schofield et al., 1975), exit interviews only have been used. This is not completely satisfactory because it does not give a record of what each user claimed to be seeking at the time he entered the library.

The great advantage of the sampling method, of course, is that it gives a reliable estimate of the failure rate, as well as permitting the usual analysis to identify the reasons for failure. Suppose that 800 users, selected at random, are briefly interviewed over a several week period as they enter the library. Of these, 510 claim to be looking for one or more "known items." Each records on a brief form whatever details he has on one of the items he is seeking. He is asked to use the same form to indicate whether or not he was able to locate the item in the catalog and whether or not he was able to locate it on the shelves. Let us say that 450 of the 510 users fully cooperate as requested and return completed forms to the investigator as they leave the library. By follow-up procedures, the investigator is able to produce the following data:

Number of items looked for	450
Number owned	364
Number of owned items located in catalog	312
Number of located items found on shelf	209
Reasons for nonavailability of item on shelf	
In circulation	62
Waiting to be reshelved	12
Misshelved	10
At binding	8
In use in the library	2
Item unaccounted for	9

Besides determining reasons for nonavailability on the shelf, this investigator has been able to show that the probability of ownership of a sought item is 364/450 (.81), the probability of a successful catalog search for an item owned is 312/364 (.86), and the probability that an item found in the catalog will be found on the shelf is 209/312 (.67). Overall, in 209 out of 450 cases (.46) the user is able to leave the library with the needed item in his hand.

Wiemers (1981) demonstrates how a survey of this kind can be extended to cover users looking for material of a particular type. For example, one indicates that he is seeking books on Scandinavian cooking. The questionnaire then determines if he was able to confirm that the library owns books on this subject and if he was able to find books on this subject on the shelf.

Examples of the use of the survey method in studies of shelf availability can be found in Urquhart and Schofield (1971, 1972), Kantor (1976), Whitlatch and Kieffer (1978), Goehlert (1978), Shaw (1980), Wood et al. (1980), Smith and Granade (1978), Gore (1975), Detweiler (1980), Frohmberg et al. (1980), and Ciliberti et al. (1987). Van House (1987) describes some procedures and presents sample survey forms.

Latent Needs

Line (1973) went beyond the typical availability survey and designed a study to determine to what extent a university library could supply bibliographic items needed by researchers *whether they consulted the library or not.*

A study of this kind might work somewhat as follows. Suppose we identify 50 faculty members willing to participate. Each is given a set of, say, 10 preprinted cards. Beginning on a selected day, a participant is to record the bibliographic details of any documents he wants or needs to consult in connection with his work at the university. One card is used for each such item and the process ends when he has used up all 10 of his cards. The cards are also designed as brief questionnaires to determine whether or not the subject actually found the item he needed, where he found it, if he is still pursuing it, and so on.

If the subjects cooperate fully, and provide reliable data, a study of this type could indicate:

1. The proportion of the document needs that the library could supply if called upon.
2. The proportion of the document needs actually converted into demands on the library's resources.
3. The success rate of the library for these demands.
4. Other sources of documents used by the faculty.
5. Types of items needed by faculty that the library could not supply.

As Line discovered, there are many problems involved in a study of this kind. In the first place the people who agree to participate may not be fully representative of the entire community. Not everyone who agrees to participate will do so, and the needs of those who cooperate may not be the same as the needs of those who do not. Line also discovered that his participants tended not to record the very simple needs—e.g., consultation of a dictionary—but only the more difficult, thus distorting the results.

This type of study is most likely to be feasible in a special library (e.g., in a small company) where the librarian knows all of the potential users. In this situation, it is possible that some form of "critical incident" technique might produce useful results. For example, a random sample of the researchers could be contacted, perhaps by telephone. Each is asked to recall the last time he needed some publication in connection with his work for the company. He is then asked if he was able to obtain it, how he obtained it, and other related questions, in an effort to determine how successful the library would be if it were the first source consulted for every need arising.

Factors Affecting Availability

The factors that affect the availability of books owned by a library have been thoroughly discussed by Buckland (1975). The most important are level of demand (popularity), number of copies, and length of loan period. It is obvious that the more popular a particular book the less likely it is to be on the shelf at any particular time. "Popularity" is not a nebulous measure in this case, but a very practical one. For example, it can be expressed in terms of a last circulation date. That is, one could say that 10% of the collection circulated at least once in the last month, 25% circulated at least once in the last six months, and so on.

It seems equally obvious that buying additional copies will improve availability. But two copies are not twice as good as one copy—sometimes both are on the shelf, sometimes one, sometimes neither—and the addition of further copies may make only a marginal difference to availability. The effect of adding an additional copy varies with the popularity of the item: if a particular book is never used it will always be available and adding a second copy does not change the situation.

If a book is off the shelf for one half of the year, one can say its availability rate is 0.5. Adding a second copy will improve availability but will not double it; two copies are not twice as good as one (Leimkuhler, 1966). Buckland (1975) presents data to show the effect of varying numbers of duplicate copies on the availability of books at different levels of popularity. With 98 demands per year for a particular title, if two copies will produce an availability rate of 0.5, three copies will improve availability to 0.7, and four copies to 0.8 (Freeman and Co., 1965).

Less obvious, perhaps, are the effects on availability of the length of the loan period. Suppose that every user of a library returns a book on or near the day on which it is due to be returned. There is, in fact, a strong tendency for this to occur, as reported by Buckland (1975) and Goehlert (1979). Then, reducing the length of the loan period from four weeks to two weeks greatly increases the probability that any book will be available on the shelf when looked for by a user. In fact, cutting the length of the period in half has roughly the same effect on availability as buying a second copy.

The librarian can improve the accessibility of books by buying more copies of popular items, reducing the length of the loan period, or both. In fact, if one wished, it would be possible to identify a desired "satisfaction level" (e.g., 0.8—a user will find a desired item to be on the shelf in eight cases out of ten) and take steps to ensure that this level would apply to every book in the library. Suppose one divided the collection into five levels of popularity on the basis of most recent circulation date. For Level 5 the probability of availability could already be 0.99 and would remain there even if the loan period for this category was extended to ten years. For Level 4 the probability of availability might already be 0.8 with a loan period of four weeks, and no further action is required. Availability for Level 3 items might be increased to 0.8 by reducing the length of the loan period from four weeks to three weeks. To reach 0.8 availability for Level 2, the length of the loan period may need to be reduced to two weeks. This leaves us with Level 1 items—the rather small number of highly popular items in the library. To ensure a probability of availability of 0.8 one might need, say, 5 copies of each and a loan period of one week.

Buckland (1975) has reported that a type of "homeostatic" effect may govern book availability. That is, if satisfaction level is pushed up from, say, 0.5 to 0.8, use of the library may increase substantially because of improved expectations of success among the community. This greatly increased demand, however, increases competition for the library's resources and forces satisfaction level down—perhaps back to 0.5. A possible solution to this would be a self-regulating library with no fixed loan period. An algorithm incorporated within an online circulation system would tell the user how long he could retain a particular book at the time he presents it for checking out. The calculation would be made on the basis of the circulation history of the book and the number of copies held, the loan period being calculated to ensure that the desired satisfaction level (say 0.8) will be maintained.

Morse (1977) shows how it is possible to calculate the probability of availability of a book given the number of circulations per year and the length of time it is absent from the shelves per circulation. He presents tables and graphs to allow one to calculate the effect on availability of increasing the number of copies or changing the loan period.

Kantor (1978) has proposed a "vitality" measure for a book collection. Vitality is the ratio of the expected failure rate, based on the proportion of the collection on loan, to the actual failure rate. Consider a collection of 100,000 volumes with 5,000 out on loan at any one time. With 5% of the collection absent from the shelves, the expected failure rate would be 5%. That is, a user could expect to find a sought item on the shelves 95% of the time. However, this assumes that all books are in equal demand, which is quite untrue. In fact, most users will be looking for high-demand items and the actual failure rate could be as high as 60%. In this example, the ratio of expected failure to actual failure is 1:12 so the vitality would be a little above 8%. Kantor claims that vitality is a good measure of the "relevance" of a collection. A decrease in vitality over time would indicate "that the library is beginning to accumulate deadwood" whereas an increase would indicate that weeding procedures have successfully eliminated some of the dead material from the library.

Study Questions

1. The Director of the XYZ Public Library (serving 100,000) would like to know how successful are the users of that library in finding particular books or other items that they seek. When an adult user walks into that library looking for a *known item*—whether book, periodical article, or whatever—what is the probability that the item will be (a) owned, (b) found by the user in the catalog, (c) on the shelf when looked for, and (d) found on the shelf by the user? How would you do a study to evaluate the performance of the library in its document delivery functions?

2. You are the director of the library of the research center of a large manufacturer. The library is intended to serve approximately 300 physicists and mathematicians at the research center. You report to the Vice President for Research. A new VP has recently been appointed. The VP feels that the library has not been sufficiently aggressive in its information services and believes that the scientists at the center have many

document needs that they do not take to the library; they either go elsewhere or perform without the information. The VP asks you to do a study to determine how many of their document needs *could be satisfied* by the library's collection, how many *are actually* satisfied by the library, and what happens to the other needs. How will you do this study?

3. Theoretically, one could design an online circulation system based on a completely flexible loan period. Using data on the number of copies of each title and the circulation history of each, the system itself would specify for how long a particular item could be borrowed by a user. The object would be to create a situation in which, no matter what book is looked for on the shelves, the chance that it would be there would rarely drop below some desired level—say a .8 probability of availability. What would be the advantages and disadvantages of such a system?

9. Factors Determining Success or Failure in Document Delivery

Chapters 2-8 have gone systematically through the steps depicted in Exhibit 2, applying various evaluation methods to the questions raised in this diagram. The present chapter pulls together and summarizes information from the earlier chapters concerning factors that determine whether or not a user can obtain a needed item during a visit to a library. These factors, shown in Exhibit 19, are divided into two broad categories:

1. Can the user find an entry for the item in the catalog?
2. Given that he finds an entry, can he find the item itself?

Before the user can find an entry, of course, the library must own a copy of the item sought and an entry for it must appear in the catalog. The underlying factors here have to do with the library's selection criteria, the librarian's knowledge of user needs, the adequacy of the budget, and various aspects of efficiency—including the time elapsing from date of publication of an item to the point at which it appears on the shelves and in the catalog.

Several important factors influence whether or not a library user can find an entry for an item in the catalog given that the entry is actually present. Some of these relate to the user's own characteristics: his intelligence, perseverance (e.g., how many cards he is willing to look through), and his experience in using catalogs in general and the present one in particular. Secondary influences, presumably, would include the quality of the guiding or labeling of the catalog (e.g., does it clearly indicate that subjects, titles, and authors appear in different sequences?) and whether or not the user has received some instruction in its use.

The single most important factor determining success or failure in catalog use is likely to be the accuracy and completeness of the information brought to the catalog by the user. Does he have the full surname of the author and is it spelled correctly? Does he have full forenames or only initials? Does he have a complete and correct title? Studies of catalog use have consistently shown that users are more likely to have complete and correct title information than complete and correct author information, although the majority will tend to search by author rather than by title. A user is more likely to be able to compensate for inaccurate or incomplete title information than for inaccurate or incomplete author information. For example, he may locate the needed entry if he has at least the first significant word of the title correct, especially if this word is rather uncommon, whereas he may fail to do so if the surname is not correct (Willis rather than Wyllys) of if he has no forenames or initials.

The significance of all of these factors, of course, will be greatly influenced by the size of the catalog. The larger the catalog, the more difficult it is to use and the more important it becomes that the user should have precise and accurate information. "R. Smith" may be adequate identification for an author in using the catalog of a school library but it may be almost useless for searching the catalog of the University of Illinois.

Another factor affecting success in the location of an entry will be the number of access points provided for an item in the catalog, including the number of cross-references (e.g., from one version or part of a name to another) and whether or not added entries are given for all book *titles*. An online catalog has obvious advantages in this respect because additional access points can usually be provided easily and economically. For example, an effective online catalog should allow access to a book through any keyword appearing in its title.

Exhibit 19 also lists "filing accuracy" and "quality of cataloging" as factors affecting the success of a user in locating an entry. While unlikely to be the most important cause of failure, misfiling might occur too often in a large catalog to be judged completely insignificant. "Quality of cataloging" refers to a whole host of factors, including the ability of a cataloger to interpret cataloging rules correctly, the logic of the rules themselves, the accuracy of the cataloger, the quality of authority files, the extent of use of "analytics," and so on. In theory, "quality" of cataloging should have a profound effect on catalog use. In practice, centralized and cooperative cataloging procedures have greatly reduced the significance of "quality" as a factor affecting the probability that a particular user will find a particular entry in a particular catalog.

The second part of Exhibit 19 relates to the probability that a user will be able to find a book or other item in the library once having located an entry for it in the catalog. This has two component probabilities: the probability that the book will be on the shelf and the probability that the user will be able to find it there.

As discussed in detail in Chapter 8, the probability of availability of a book is controlled by three major factors: its level of popularity, the

Can user find entry?

Does library own copy?

Has it been cataloged?

Can user locate in catalog?

    Familiarity with catalog
    User's intelligence and
      perseverance
    Quality of cataloging
    Number of access points
    Quality and completeness of
     information brought to
     catalog by user
    Filing accuracy
    Size and complexity of catalog

Can user find copy?

Is it on the shelf?

    Popularity of item
    Number of copies
    Length of loan period
    Security factors

Can user find it on the shelf?

    User's ability to transcribe
     or remember call numbers
    Number of shelf sequences
    Quality of guiding
    Accuracy of shelving

Amount and quality of staff assistance available

Exhibit 19

Major factors affecting success of document delivery

number of copies owned, and the length of the loan period. An additional factor is that of the level of security in the library. A very high rate of loss within a library could have a significant impact on availability since it is the items of greatest popularity that are most likely to be missing.

If a book is not in use, it should be on the shelf and available to be used. This is not always the case. Books may be absent from the shelves to allow them to be rebound or they may be waiting to be reshelved. It is inevitable that some loss of availability due to these causes will occur but it can be minimized if the library operates efficiently. Books should be reshelved as soon as possible after they have been used within the library or returned from circulation, and the librarian must avoid sending materials to the bindery while they are known to be in great demand.

Even if a book is "on the shelf," this does not guarantee that the user will find it. It might be misplaced on the shelf, or the user may miss it because of a confusing multiplicity of shelving sequences, because the shelves are inadequately labeled, or because of physical conditions—shelves too high, shelves too low, lighting inadequate in the stacks, call number on spine obliterated, and so on. Finally, a user might not find a book because he fails to remember or to transcribe its call number correctly.

One other factor is given prominence in Exhibit 19. It is assumed that the amount and quality of the staff assistance available will influence many of the other factors listed: a staff member should be available to help a user who is having difficulty in finding an entry in the catalog or a book on the shelves.

Chapters 2-9 have dealt in some detail with various facets of evaluation applied to document delivery. Evaluation of the major components of reference service is the subject of Chapter 10 and 11.

Study Questions

1. Does Exhibit 19 present a comprehensive list of factors affecting success in document delivery? If not, what is omitted?

2. Try to redraw Exhibit 2 (Chapter 1) in such a way that all the factors listed in Exhibit 19 are present. Try to put the factors in the sequence in which they would affect the search for a known item.

10. Question Answering

This chapter deals with the evaluation of one major aspect of reference service in libraries—the answering of factual-type questions. This activity can be examined in several different ways: the number of questions received and their types, the distribution of questions by time of day and day of week, time taken to answer questions, staffing requirements, sources used to answer questions, and so on. However, a true evaluation would attempt to determine how many of the questions posed to the library are answered completely and correctly.*

The situation is illustrated in Exhibit 20. To get a complete picture of the quality of this service in some library, one would need to know how many questions were received in a particular period of time, how many were attempted (some might be rejected—legitimately or not—because they are out of scope, of a type that the library refuses to answer as a matter of policy, or are judged to require an inordinate amount of time to answer), for how many of the attempted questions an answer was found, and for how many of these was the answer complete and correct. If the library refers the questioner to another agency (or individual), the library can be considered successful if the agency referred to is able to provide the needed information (see Crowley [1984] for the results of a study on the ability of a regional referral center to answer questions posed to it by local public libraries).

In the normal course of events, the library will not have all of the data implicit in the diagram. It is most likely to record and retain data on the number of questions attempted and on the number for which some kind of answer is supplied. Certainly, it will not know how many of the questions were answered correctly. Thus, when the annual report of some library claims that the reference department "answered 95% of all questions received," it probably means merely that some kind of answer was found for 95% of the questions attempted.

The hypothetical data of Exhibit 20 indicate that a user asking the library to find the answer to a question faces about a 68% chance (.95 x .90 x.80) that this question will be answered completely and correctly. However, those evaluations that have been performed suggest that the

---

*Notice that "user satisfaction," in this situation, is a somewhat different criterion. A user may be "satisfied" with an answer that is incomplete or incorrect because he does not know, at that point, that the information received is faulty.

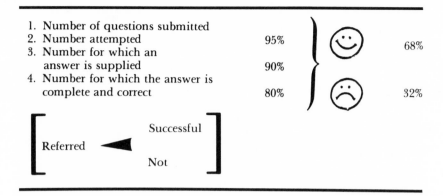

1. Number of questions submitted
2. Number attempted   95%
3. Number for which an
   answer is supplied   90%
4. Number for which the answer is
   complete and correct   80%

68%

32%

Referred ◀ Successful / Not

Exhibit 20

Data needed for a complete evaluation of question-answering activities

actual probability of success may be lower than this—that less than 60% of the questions received by public libraries may be answered completely and correctly.

How can this aspect of reference service be evaluated objectively? One way would be to incorporate the study into a larger evaluation of library services based on interviews with a random sample of library users. Thus, if a user entering the library claims to be seeking the answer to some factual-type question, that question is recorded by the investigator. On leaving the library, the user is asked to indicate whether or not he has an answer, what that answer is, and how it was found (by the librarian, by the user with the librarian's help, by the user unaided).

There is no real reason why such a procedure would not work, and it may provide valuable data that the library can use to make improvements in its services. However, it does have a number of disadvantages:

1. A lot of time would have to be spent to determine unequivocally whether or not the answer supplied is correct.
2. Members of the reference staff will know that the evaluation is taking place, and may find themselves trying harder on the survey days than they do at other times.
3. In a public library, at least, it is likely that more questions will come to the library by telephone than by personal visit. There is no way of identifying users who submit requests by telephone. Moreover, the types of questions thus submitted may not be exactly the same as those made by personal visit and the probability of receiving a correct answer may also differ.

On the whole, then, the best way to evaluate question-answering services is through some form of simulation.

Simulations

In order to perform a simulation, it is necessary to collect and use a group of questions for which definitive answers have already been established. The reference staff of the library under scrutiny can then be evaluated according to two possible criteria:

1. How many of these questions they are able to answer completely and correctly.
2. How many of the questions they answer completely and correctly out of those they *could* answer because the library is known to own at least one source containing a definitive answer.

In the latter case, the evaluator must carefully establish whether or not the library owns a source containing the correct answer for each test question.

The questions used in such a study must obviously be typical of the questions put to the library being evaluated in the normal course of events; otherwise the information gathered will not be relevant to the library under study. They will usually be real questions collected from other libraries having similar characteristics to the one being studied. If the questions are to be used to *compare* the performance of several libraries, care must be taken to ensure that they are capable of discriminating among libraries. This requires that they be pretested in another group of libraries. The questions that all libraries get correct and those that no library gets correct should both be eliminated since neither group can discriminate among libraries (Crowley and Childers, 1971). Test questions should always be pretested, however they are to be used, to ensure that they are unambiguous.

A simulation study of question answering can be performed obtrusively or unobtrusively. In the obtrusive study, the staff members participating know they are being evaluated and have agreed to take part. A librarian is given a set of, say, 20 questions and is evaluated in terms of how many are answered satisfactorily. The evaluator may be present while the librarian is working, perhaps recording the time taken to answer each question (an alternative is to establish an absolute time limit—the librarian is to answer as many as possible in the time available) and/or to observe how the librarian works, which sources are consulted, and so on.

Clearly, this approach suffers the disadvantages of obtrusive studies in general. Knowing they are observed, the subjects may not operate in quite the same way that they would under more normal conditions. Some may be excited by the challenge and do rather better than they would otherwise, while others may become nervous and perform below their true capabilities.* On the other hand, the evaluator can learn things from the obtrusive study (e.g., on search strategy) that would be difficult to learn in an unobtrusive study.

Some obtrusive studies have focused on how the reference librarian works rather than on the outcome of the task (Carlson, 1964; Torr et al., 1966). In studies of this kind, the investigator may accompany the reference librarian, as he goes from source to source, performing in effect a running interview. Alternatively, the librarian may be asked to use a microphone to record his thoughts and search strategy as he seeks the answer to a more complex question.

Unobtrusive Studies

In the unobtrusive study, the questions collected for the test are submitted to the library in such a way that they are accepted as "real" questions by "real" users. Once more, the library is evaluated on the basis of how many of these questions are answered completely and correctly.

Volunteers—for example, students of library science—are used to submit the questions to the library, usually by telephone. A schedule is established that specifies that a particular question is to be submitted to a particular library during a selected time slot on a selected day. This is to ensure that the test questions do not arouse suspicion, as they might if they were all concentrated within a short period of time, and that they are applied during a variety of "environmental" conditions (a question received during a very quiet period in the library may be treated differently from one arriving in a particularly hectic period).

The volunteers ("surrogate users") may be asked to record more than the answer they receive to a question. For example, they may record details of their conversation with the librarian, including their impressions of his or her helpfulness and whether or not they were asked to clarify the question, how long it took the librarian to find the answer, and whether or not the librarian quoted the source from which the answer was supplied.

The volunteers used in such a study must be carefully trained. They must present the question in a natural way, must understand it, and must be ready to indicate why they need the answer should they be asked for this information.

---

*Weech and Goldhor (1982) present some evidence that reference librarians perform better when they know they are being evaluated.

Special problems are posed when questions are submitted by a long distance telephone call, which might be necessary if the study embraces a whole group of libraries. If the librarian discovers that the call is from another town, he may legitimately ask why or even refuse to handle the question. Suspicion may be aroused when the questioner refuses to leave a telephone number and, instead, asks to call the library back. The types of problems that can arise in a study of this kind have been well reviewed by Childers (1972) and by Hernon and McClure (1987).

In principle, there is no reason why an unobtrusive study cannot be done by having the volunteers make personal visits to the libraries. However, for evaluation purposes this is not quite as "clean" as the telephone situation for the librarian may direct the questioner to a reference book rather than supplying the answer.

In performing an unobtrusive study, the investigator must establish clearcut rules as to how each question is to be scored. For the question "When did Christian IV of Denmark die?" the answer is unequivocally 1648. On the other hand, consider the question "When was Geoffrey Chaucer born?" One library might answer "1340," while another might respond "It is thought to be about 1340 but it is not known for sure." If the second answer is correct, does the first library get any "points" for its answer? Another factor is whether or not the librarian quotes the source from which an answer is drawn. An answer with source supplied may be considered more complete than one with no source supplied.

A number of evaluations of reference service have been performed by means of simulations in the last twenty years, including:

Bunge (1967), an obtrusive study in medium-size public libraries in the Midwest

Goldhor (1967), an obtrusive study involving 10 questions and 12 public libraries

The Institute for the Advancement of Medical Communication (Pizer and Cain, 1968), two types of obtrusive study performed in academic medical libraries

Crowley and Childers (1971), two separate unobtrusive studies of public libraries in New Jersey

King and Berry (1973), a pilot study (unobtrusive) of telephone information service at the University of Minnesota libraries

Powell (1976), an obtrusive study involving public libraries in Illinois (see Benham and Powell [1987])

Childers (1978), an unobtrusive evaluation of public libraries in Suffolk County, New York

Ramsden (1978), an unobtrusive study of public libraries in Melbourne, Australia

Schmidt (1980) an unobtrusive study of college libraries in New South Wales, with some of the questions posed by telephone and some by personal visit.

Myers and Jirjees (1983), two separate unobtrusive studies involving academic libraries

McClure and Hernon (1983), an unobtrusive evaluation of reference service involving government documents collections in academic libraries

Rodger and Goodwin (1984), a study of accuracy of reference service at the Fairfax County Public Library

Gers and Seward (1985), a major study among public libraries in Maryland: 40 questions posed to 60 outlets of 22 public library systems (2400 questions in all, half submitted by telephone and half by personal visit)

Birbeck (1986), a large unobtrusive study involving 15 questions and 24 public libraries in England

Benham (1987), an unobtrusive study involving recent graduates of accredited library schools.

Several of these studies have been reviewed or summarized by Powell (1984) and Crowley (1985).

These various investigations display numerous differences. Some were applied obtrusively, some unobtrusively. In some, the questions were submitted by telephone, in some by personal visit, in some by a mixture of the two techniques. Some studies involved public libraries, other academic. In a few cases, the study was performed to test some hypothesis (e.g., that staff members with one type of background would outperform others or that the size of the reference collection would have a significant influence on the probability that a question would be answered correctly).

At the same time, all the studies have something important in common: they show that the user of a library faces a surprisingly low probability that his factual question will be answered accurately. Overall, the studies tend to support a probability in the range of 50 to 60%, with some libraries or groups of libraries doing much worse than this, and a few doing rather better.*

Weech and Goldhor (1982) were able to compare the obtrusive and unobtrusive approaches in five public libraries in Illinois, using two

---

*In Childers' study of 20 questions in 57 libraries (Childers, 1978), one library got only 15% right while another scored as high as 75%.

sets of fifteen questions, each set being considered comparable in terms of difficulty. They recorded an overall score of 70% accuracy for the unobtrusive study and 85% for the obtrusive study, both scores measurably higher than those recorded in other studies of public libraries.

The Weech and Goldhor study was performed at the Library Research Center, Graduate School of Library and Information Science, University of Illinois. For a number of years this center also performed an annual survey of selected public libraries in Illinois, using students from the University to put two questions to their own libraries while at home on vacation, one question in person, and one by telephone. The results are incorporated with other results (e.g., on document availability) in an annual Index of Quality for Illinois public libraries (Wallace, 1983).

The answering of factual-type questions is not the only aspect of reference service that can or should be evaluated. Olson (1984) points out that, in addition, reference librarians should be evaluated on their responses to questions involving knowledge of library services,* on their performance in providing instruction in use of reference sources, and on their ability to "negotiate" a question. She goes on to suggest how such studies might be performed. Another reference service that is becoming increasingly important and prevalent involves the conduct of literature searches for users via data bases accessible online. The evaluation of literature searching is discussed in the next chapter.

Another type of obtrusive reference test involves the evaluation of the reference librarian on his ability to correct an incomplete or erroneous bibliographic citation (Orr and Olson, 1968).

If the staff of a library is evaluated, obtrusively or unobtrusively, on its ability to answer reference questions, the study should be performed with the intention of improving the service and not as a mere intellectual exercise. That is, the evaluator should attempt to identify the most important factors influencing the quality of the reference service in order to make recommendations—on the collection, training of staff, recruitment of staff, allocation of staff time, or whatever—on how the service might be improved. The remainder of this chapter will be devoted to factors affecting the quality of question-answering services in libraries.

---

*The Fairfax County, Virginia, study reported by Rodger and Goodwin (1984) found evidence that reference librarians do not always display adequate knowledge of library services.

Performance Factors*

Exhibit 21 relates to the probability that questions will arise in the minds of members of a community and that these individuals will approach a library to have their questions answered. An underlying assumption is that a library is readily accessible to members of the community.

It seems reasonable to suppose that level of education and intelligence, as well as diversity of professional and personal interests, will strongly affect the probability that questions will arise in the minds of individuals, information be needed by them, and information needs actually be recognized.** These same factors also seem likely to influence motivation, i.e., whether or not an individual actually seeks to find the answer to some question.

There are at least two other factors likely to influence motivation. The first is the perceived value of having a question answered. In many cases, an answer will have no financial value. Nevertheless, it will have some intangible value to the questioner, such as curiosity satisfied or mind set at rest. Even if the reward is intangible, when an individual seeks the answer to a question, he or she is making a type of value judgment: that the answer is worth the effort (a cost) of pursuing.

In some instances, of course, an answer will have financial value. In these situations, the amount of money involved will probably determine the motivation. For example, in buying a major appliance, such as a refrigerator, one could save $100 or more by finding that some consumer magazine judges one brand as effective as another. In buying an electric toaster, on the other hand, one may decide that the potential savings are so small that the consumer information is not worth the effort of seeking.

Finally, although no hard evidence exists on this, one suspects that the motivation to find an answer to some question will be influenced by the individual's perception of the probability that an answer exists, is recorded, and can be found. The answers to many questions may never be sought because the individuals, in whose minds the questions are raised, believe (perhaps quite erroneously) that no recorded answers exist.

---

*This section is a somewhat modified and expanded version of an article that first appeared in *The Reference Librarian* in 1984 and is published here with the permission of the editor of the journal.

**These factors seem to apply more to an individual in a "home" environment. In a business environment, presumably, somewhat different factors will apply.

Sequence of events	Factors affecting probability that event will occur
1. Question arises in the mind of some individual.	Individual's education, background, interests, experience, and level of intelligence and literacy.
2. Individual recognizes that he needs to have question answered.	Individual's education, background, interests, experience, and level of intelligence and literacy.
3. Individual is sufficiently motivated to seek answer.	As for Event 1, plus: (a) the value of the answer to the individual, and (b) the individual's perception of the probability that the question can be answered by some source.
4. Individual approaches library to have question answered.	Is individual aware of existence of library? Is individual aware that library provides this service? Is library perceived to be appropriate and convenient source to use? Has individual had good or bad experiences with libraries in general and this library in particular? Is the library open at the time answer is needed? Can individual visit or contact library at time answer is needed?

Exhibit 21

Probability that a question will arise and be submitted to a library

The next step illustrated in Exhibit 21 relates to the probability that an individual, once decided to seek the answer to some question, will go to a library rather than to some other source. Clearly, he must know that a library exists, that he is qualified to use it, and that the library does attempt to find answers to many types of question. If these conditions apply, the library will presumably be selected if (a) the questioner perceives the library to be the most convenient information source to use, (b) he retains favorable impressions if he has used the library in the past, and (c) the library is open at the time the information is needed.

Given that it is approached by some member of the community, will the library seek to find the answer to his question? Clearly, the question must first be understood by the librarian receiving it. Whether this occurs will depend on the ability of both librarian and questioner to communicate. If the question is understood by the librarian, will it be accepted? Perhaps the questioner will be refused because he is not a qualified user (e.g., in the case of some industrial library). If the questioner is acceptable, the question may not be. It could be of a type that the library, as a matter of policy, refuses to answer (e.g., homework questions, quiz questions, or certain kinds of medical questions). See Exhibit 22.

---

1. Communication factors:
    Questioner
    Librarian
2. Policy factors:
    Is questioner acceptable to library?
    Is question acceptable to library?

Exhibit 22
Will library attempt to find answer?

For some questions, while an answer may be considered to "exist," at least in a theoretical sense, it has not been recorded or even, perhaps, determined. This might apply, for example, to a question on the height of a relatively obscure building or one on the thermal conductivity of some uncommon alloy. Given that an answer has been recorded somewhere, the question arises as to whether or not the librarian can locate it. Six groups of factors influencing this probability are identified in Exhibit 23 and elaborated on in Exhibits 24-29.

---

1. Is answer recorded somewhere?
2. Can librarian find answer?
    Policy factors
    Collection factors
    Librarian factors
    Question-related factors
    User factors
    Environmental factors

Exhibit 23
Will questioner receive a complete and correct answer?

1. How much time is librarian willing and able to spend?
2. What expenditures can librarian incur?
   Long-distance telephone
   Access to online sources

Exhibit 24

Policy factors

1. Does the library own a source that contains the complete and correct answer?

2. How many sources does the library own that contain a complete and correct answer?

3. How accessible are these sources to the librarian?

4. How well organized and indexed are these sources?

Exhibit 25

Collection factors

1. Knowledge:
   Of collection
   General knowledge
      Current awareness
      Language abilities

2. Ability and willingness to communicate

3. Decision-making abilities

4. Perception of professional responsibilities and commitment to these responsibilities

5. Efficiency:
   Speed
   Accuracy

6. Education and training

7. Experience as a librarian and as a reference librarian

Exhibit 26

Librarian factors

Most questions can be answered if one is willing to put enough time, energy, and money into the endeavor. Whether a particular user

1. Subject
2. Obscurity
3. Complexity
4. Stability of answer (in particular, how recently did
   answer change?)

Exhibit 27

Question-related factors

1. Status
2. Personality and attitude
3. Ability to comprehend answer

Exhibit 28

User factors

1. Stress
2. Physical/mental health of librarian
3. Pure environmental:
   Temperature
   Humidity
   Lighting

Exhibit 29

Environmental factors

gets a non-routine question answered completely and correctly will partly depend on how much time the librarian is willing and able to devote to it. This will be determined in part by library policy. But other factors also come into play: how busy the librarian is at the time the question arises, how important the librarian perceives the questioner to be, how interested the librarian is in the question (and, under certain circumstances, the questioner!), and so on.

There are other library policies affecting the probability that a question will be answered completely and correctly. An important one relates to how money can be spent. In some cases, the most up-to-date or accurate information could be obtained through a long-distance telephone call. In other cases, such a call might save many minutes of the librarian's time. Exactly the same could be said of access to online data bases and data banks. Library policies are very shortsighted if they do not allow reference librarians to use the most cost-effective approach available. Regrettably, in most libraries, ownership represents a more legitimate expenditure of public funds than access does.

It seems fairly obvious that a question is more likely to be answered if the library owns a source that could provide the answer than if it does not. Some of the other collection factors identified in Exhibit 25 may be somewhat less obvious.

It is hypothesized (without any hard data to offer in support*) that the probability that a question will be answered completely and correctly increases with the number of sources owned by the library in which the answer is recorded. This is really a matter of probability: the more substitutable sources that exist, the greater the probability that the librarian will use one of them. This probability is related to the relative obscurity, or otherwise, of the question. "What is the capital of Argentina?" is a question that could be answered by any one of several hundred sources in some libraries. On the other hand, consider the following question: "What is the origin of the name Tigre, a resort close to Buenos Aires?" This question can be answered by few (if any) sources in even a large library. The probability that this question would be answered correctly is very low.

Another hypothesis, untested as far as this author is aware, is that the physical accessibility of the information source to the librarian influences the probability that an answer will be found. In many libraries, a "quick-reference" collection exists immediately adjacent to the reference desk. If the correct answer to a question is contained here, it seems highly probable that the librarian will find it. This probability is likely to decrease successively when: the answer exists elsewhere in the open-access reference collection, the answer exists in reference materials in closed-access stacks, the answer exists in circulating materials, the answer exists in a circulating item that is now on loan, the answer exists in an item in a remote storage facility.

Finally, the organization of the information source needs to be taken into account. For example, for a particular question the only

---

*Powell (1976) studied the relationship between collection size and success in answering questions in the aggregate. He did not determine number of possible sources for each question.

answer may exist in one history of art. The probability that this answer
will be found by a librarian, given that the book itself is looked at, will
depend on how the book is organized and how well it is indexed.

In Exhibit 25, collection factors are considered from the aspect of a
single factual question. Primary factors, rather than secondary, are
identified. Such factors as "size of collection" are purely secondary
since, viewed at the level of the individual question, these factors merely
influence the primary factors (e.g., the probability that the library will
own multiple information sources that are equally complete and
correct).

A number of librarian factors are identified in Exhibit 26; some are
more important than others. First and foremost, the librarian must have
a detailed knowledge of the information sources available. However,
general knowledge is not insignificant. In particular, the librarian
should have a good grasp of current events. Without this, he may well
give an answer that is no longer accurate (e.g., to the question "Who is
the world record holder in the 1500 metres?" when the record was broken
two days before the question was asked). Ability to read foreign lan-
guages may be important in some libraries but, for most questions, is
not likely to be a major factor influencing the probability that an answer
will be found.

The ability of the librarian to communicate effectively influences
his understanding of the question in the first place as well as his ability
to convey a correct answer to the user. Decision-making abilities affect
the efficiency of the librarian's search strategy. Other important decisions include: when to refer to an outside source and when to give up
completely.

The librarian's perception of his professional responsibilities may
influence whether or not he accepts a question (e.g., questions should
not be rejected out-of-hand because they seem too difficult) as well as
how much time he is willing to devote to it.

The efficiency of the librarian is another important factor. The
more quickly he finds answers to the routine questions, the more time
he can devote to the nonroutine. He must also be accurate, in checking
indexes, in reading text or tables of data, and in relaying answers to
users.

Certainly one would expect that, all other things being equal, the
more experienced the librarian in reference work, the more likely the
question to be answered completely and correctly. To a lesser extent, one
might also expect this probability to be related to the education and
training of the librarian, although a study by Bunge (1967) tended to
indicate that reference librarians without formal education (i.e., without

attending library school) were no less likely to answer questions correctly than those with formal education in librarianship.*

The complexity of a question (Exhibit 27) will affect the probability that the librarian will understand it, that a complete and correct answer can be found, and that the answer can be transmitted successfully to the user. The obscurity of the question will affect the number of sources in which an answer appears and, thus, the probability that an answer will be found. The subject matter involved, since this relates to the strengths and weaknesses of particular collections, as well as of particular librarians, is another significant factor.

More important than all of these, however, may be the stability of the answer and, more particularly, how recently the answer changed. The question "When was Smetana's *The Bartered Bride* first performed in the United States?" is orders of magnitude more easy to answer correctly than "When was *The Bartered Bride* performed most recently by a major opera company in the United States?" The first answer, presumably, cannot change while the second may have changed as recently as yesterday.

While some librarians may deny it, it is hard to believe that "human" factors do not enter into this picture (Exhibit 28). In an industrial library, a vice president receives more care and time than a design engineer recently appointed. In an academic health science library, the same situation applies to the dean of the medical school.

But status is not the only "human" influence. Whether consciously or unconsciously, it seems reasonable to suppose that a librarian will try harder for the questioner judged "simpatico" (or, for that matter, "simpatica") than for one considered rude, arrogant, or ignorant.

Finally, although an answer may exist, and the librarian can comprehend it, the user may not be able to. This might apply, for example, in the case of a questioner who is a child. Alternatively, the librarian may locate a source for the answer but neither the librarian nor user can understand it. For example, the user may be a practicing engineer and the answer, appearing in the literature of applied mechanics, is incomprehensible to him because it is too mathematical.

Environmental factors (Exhibit 29) may be more important than they seem at first sight. If a questioner calls at 9:05, shortly after the library has opened, it may be more likely that his question is answered correctly than if he calls at 12:05 at which time two of the three reference librarians are at lunch, five people are waiting at the reference desk, and

---

*However, the less trained staff members took longer to answer questions.

two telephones are ringing. Stress influences the accuracy of the librarian, his effectiveness, and his perseverance.*

Quite apart from these stress factors, the efficiency of librarians varies from one day to the next depending on health factors, how much sleep they have had, whether or not they have quarrelled with their spouses that day, and a whole host of related factors that are frequently overlooked and are difficult to categorize. Also frequently overlooked is the fact that human efficiency diminishes as physical environmental conditions deteriorate. In a building without air conditioning, time of day may significantly influence the probability that a question will be answered correctly.

Exhibit 30 relates to the probability that a librarian, unable to answer a question himself, will refer the library user to another source. One factor has to do with the librarian's own self-assurance. Some librarians seem reluctant to refer a questioner elsewhere, especially to another professional colleague or department, because they feel that such an action is a sign of their own incompetence. Others may refuse to refer because they adopt a tenacious and proprietary interest in a particular question. Tenacity is an admirable quality not if it results in failure to answer an answerable question.**

1. Is librarian willing to refer question
   (a) to a colleague in the library,
   (b) to an outside source?

2. How extensive is the librarian's knowledge of the resources, abilities, and interests of individuals or institutions?

3. Do referral directories appropriate to this question exist, does the library own them (or can access them online), and does the librarian know of them?

4. Is the questioner willing to be referred?

Exhibit 30
Referral factors

*Nevertheless, based on the study of public libraries in Maryland, Gers and Seward (1985) claim that degree of "busyness" seems not to influence the probability that a question will be answered correctly.

**In a study of public libraries in Illinois, Wallace (1983) discovered some reluctance to refer a question to system resources when the reference librarian was unable to answer it locally.

If the librarian is willing to refer, the quality of his referral will depend on his knowledge of primary or secondary information sources, as well as the relevance and accessibility of these sources and the willingness of the questioner to be referred elsewhere. Once the question is referred, of course, all of the performance factors previously identified will tend to apply to the new situation.

Not all the factors listed, obviously, are of equal importance. Their range and diversity do indicate, however, that the effectiveness of question-answering activities is governed by a rather complex set of variables. Moreover, chance enters into the situation: if one telephones a public library, for example, the probability that one's factual question will be answered completely and correctly may depend on the time selected and how the reference librarian happens to be feeling that day. It is little wonder that several studies have indicated that the probability of complete success in this situation may not be much more than .5 to .6. On the other hand, it should also be recognized that the factors identified imply some redundancy and counterbalancing. For example, that a particular question can be answered correctly from several sources might tend to compensate for the fact that a librarian may not be feeling at his very best on a certain day.

As a result of a large study performed among public libraries in Maryland, Gers and Seward (1985) report that "behavioral factors" seem to exert more influence on reference performance than any other type of factor. As Travillian (1985) notes, four behavioral factors correlated with completeness and correctness of response:

1. The level of negotiation of the question.
2. Whether or not the librarian used a follow-up question to determine if the questioner was satisfied with the response.
3. The degree of interest shown by the librarian.
4. The extent to which the librarian seemed to be "comfortable" in dealing with the questioner.

Correctness of response did not seem to correlate with size of collection, size of staff, or the extent to which the staff appeared to be "busy" at the time the question was received.

In terms of factors affecting the performance of reference service, the results of the Maryland study must be viewed with considerable caution. More than half the questions used could be answered from a single source (*World Almanac*) and 87.5% could be answered using only seven basic reference tools. It is hardly surprising, then, that size of collection did not correlate with quality of reference service.

As electronic information sources are increasingly used to support question-answering activities, the importance of some of these factors will decline. Clearly, access will be more important than ownership and the size and redundancy of the collection will no longer be significant variables affecting the quality of reference service. Moreover, online indexes to the contents of electronic resources will tend to ensure that a librarian will choose the best source for any particular question. At the same time, the ease with which an electronic source can be updated will tend to ensure that the information is the most current available.

Study Questions

1. When a student or faculty member walks into the Reference Room at the University of Illinois Library, looking for the answer to a factual question, what is the probability that he or she will find or receive a complete and correct answer? How would you determine this probability?

2. The Nevada State Library wishes to establish a "state reference library" to act as a backup for reference services provided by public libraries throughout the state. The proposed state-supported library would be the first source each public library would contact for most factual reference questions they are unable to answer from their own resources. Rather than establishing a completely new library, the State Librarian has decided that the new reference resource should be located within an existing public library and that State funds should be spent to strengthen the reference collection of the library chosen, as well as to provide additional staff. There are two problems:

1) Which public library should be chosen? The contenders are those in Las Vegas and Reno.
2) To what extent should the collection be expanded? From a cost-effectiveness viewpoint, how large should the reference collection be? The goal is a service capable of answering 95% of the questions referred to it by other libraries.

What data would you collect, and how would you collect them, in order to advise the State Librarian on which public library to choose and on the optimum size for the expanded reference collection?

3. Have *all* the factors affecting success/failure in question answering been identified in this chapter? If not, what is omitted? Try to draw a diagram (similar to that of Exhibit 2) in which all of these factors are presented. Can they be presented in a sequence that reflects the order in which they might affect the probability that a particular question will be answered completely and correctly?

11. Evaluation of Literature Searching Services

This chapter discusses the evaluation of those information services that respond to a user's request for "information" on some topic by searching data bases (printed or electronic) to identify bibliographic items that appear to deal with this topic. Such services are sometimes referred to as "bibliographic searching" or "information retrieval" services.

It is only in the last twenty years that information services of this kind have become fairly common in most types of libraries. Earlier, these services could be found only in certain special libraries, particularly those in industry. In general, public, school, and academic libraries lacked the resources to attempt anything but the simplest of bibliographic searches for their users. Instead, they generally preferred to direct users to appropriate printed sources in which they could perform their own searches, also instructing them in the use of these sources if necessary.

This situation has changed dramatically since early in the 1970s. The use of online networks to search bibliographic data bases is now commonplace in academic and special libraries of all sizes as well as in some of the larger public libraries.

A rather complex set of interrelationships now exists among the various actors—individual and institutional—on the online searching scene. A somewhat simplified view of these relationships is presented in Exhibit 31. The *producer* plays key roles in the whole operation as compiler and publisher of the data base. Compilation involves the acquisition of published materials within the stated scope of the data base (which implies careful selection criteria) and the processing of these to form bibliographic representations (records) within the data base. This may involve descriptive cataloging, subject indexing (perhaps using terms drawn from a controlled vocabulary such as a thesaurus), and sometimes the writing of abstracts. In some cases, however, the intellectual processing is minimized: key words in titles and abstracts are used as access points in place of humanly assigned index terms. Most frequently today, the data base is distributed in two versions: in machine-readable (electronic) form and as a printed index (with or without abstracts) roughly equivalent to the electronic form.

Machine-readable data bases are acquired by various *computer centers*. These centers have developed software to convert all data bases

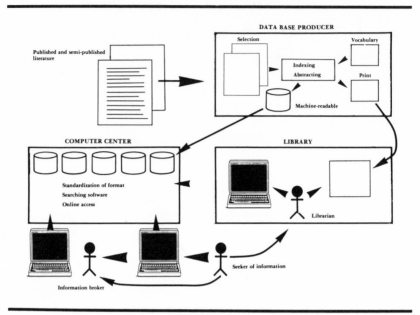

Exhibit 31
Online searching situation in the United States

to a common processing format, to make them accessible online via various telecommunications networks, and to allow them to be interrogated by remote users. *Libraries* generally access these data bases through one or more of these computer centers although, in a few cases, the data base producer may also make online access possible through computers of its own.

The *seeker of information* may visit a library to ask the librarian to perform a search on his behalf; this will usually be done online although it could also involve use of data bases in printed form housed within the library itself. Alternatively, the user could visit the library to perform his own search in printed tools or (less common) to use the library's terminals to access data bases directly. As terminals become increasingly available in offices and in homes, it seems likely that more and more individuals will perform their own online searches without the help of a librarian. Indeed, some special libraries now prefer to train users to perform their own searches instead of performing searches on their behalf.

Finally, rather than going to a library or performing searches for themselves, some individuals or institutions may prefer to use the services of an *information broker* who will conduct searches of data bases on a fee basis.

For present purposes it will be assumed that a library user asks a librarian to perform an online search to satisfy some *information need*. The obvious evaluation question is "To what extent do the results of the search satisfy the information need?"

Evaluation Criteria

The criteria that are appropriate to the evaluation of the results of a literature search will vary somewhat depending on the type of information need. Three broad types can be identified:

1. The user wants to find out if anything has been written on a particular subject and will be satisfied to find a single item on this subject.*
2. The user wants to retrieve a selection of representative items on a subject but does not need to find everything.
3. The user wants a comprehensive search—everything on the subject should be retrieved.

A fourth type of need also exists but occurs very infrequently: the user believes that nothing has been published on some topic and sets out to prove it. Of the three principal types of need enumerated above, the second is probably more common than the third and the first is least common.

An obvious evaluation criterion, applicable to all of these cases, is whether or not the search retrieves one or more items that the requester finds useful in satisfying his information need. For the second type of need and, more particularly, the third, the criterion is extended to "how many useful items were found?" The term *pertinent* will be used henceforth to refer to an item that is useful to the user in that it contributes to the satisfaction of his information need. (Considerable discussion exists in the literature on the meaning of the terms *pertinence* and *relevance* and on the difference between the two—see, for example, Lancaster (1979) and Swanson (1986)—and this will not be repeated here.)

The retrieval of pertinent items from the data base is frequently referred to as *recall* and the extent to which pertinent items are retrieved as a *recall ratio*. Thus, if a data base contains 12 items pertinent to a

---

*A search of a data base may also be performed in order to answer some factual question. In this case, the evaluation criteria are the same as those applying to other question-answering situations (see Chapter 10).

particular need and a search in this data base retrieves 9 of the 12, one could say that the *recall ratio* is 9/12, or .75.

Recall alone gives a very incomplete picture of how efficient a search has been. For example, it might be acceptable to find 9 pertinent items among 20 items retrieved but quite unacceptable to find 9 among 200. The former search has performed at much greater *precision* than the latter. A *precision ratio* is frequently used in conjunction with the recall ratio to give an indication of how efficient or discriminating a search has been. Thus, in the examples used earlier, one could say that .75 recall had been achieved at .45 precision (probably quite acceptable) or at .045 precision (probably unacceptable).

In a sense, the precision ratio provides a rather indirect measure of the "cost" of a search to a user: it will take much more time to examine a printout of 200 items to find 9 useful than to find 9 among 20. Clearly, if the user is paying for the search, a more direct measure of cost can be used, namely the cost per pertinent item retrieved. Suppose that the search that achieved a precision of 9/20 cost the user $12, while the search that achieved 9/200 cost $30. In one case the cost per pertinent item is $1.33; in the other it is $3.33.

The cost per pertinent item retrieved is related to both the recall ratio and the precision ratio. Obviously, a search that retrieves 18 pertinent items at $12 is "twice as good" as one that retrieves 9 at $12. Less obvious, perhaps, is that a precision ratio of 9/200 implies a greater cost than a precision ratio of 9/20. This is because the higher precision suggests a more direct search approach requiring less time at the terminal. It also indicates lower printout costs, especially when a charge is levied for each citation printed. In other words, the better the search, in terms of recall and precision, the lower the cost is likely to be per pertinent item retrieved.

In the discussion so far it has been assumed that a librarian performs a search for a user and delivers the results in the form of a printout of bibliographic references. The cost per pertinent item retrieved will be equally applicable to a situation in which the library user performs his own search, even if no printout is made. In this case, also, recall and precision will affect the cost per pertinent item retrieved.

So far, three different performance measures have been mentioned: recall ratio, precision ratio, and cost per pertinent item retrieved. Many others have been suggested or used (Robertson, 1969), including the complements of the recall ratio (which can be thought of as a *miss ratio*) and the precision ratio (a *noise ratio* or *noise factor*) and the *expected search length* (W.S. Cooper, 1968). Some of these other measures are more "mathematically acceptable" than recall/precision, and are especially valuable in experimental situations in which different retrieval systems or retrieval approaches are being compared (Sparck Jones, 1981). Nevertheless, the three measures discussed are those that most directly indicate the value and/or acceptability of a search in the eyes of the library user.

Application of the Criteria

Suppose one wants to evaluate the literature searching activities of a particular library, say a departmental library within a university. It will be important to get feedback on a continuous basis from all users of the service so that some form of quality control is in effect. A brief evaluation form should accompany each search printout delivered to a user, the user being urged to return the completed form when the results have been examined. The form should obtain the user's subjective assessment of the value of the search as a whole, using some scale (such as: of great value, of value, of little value, of no value), as well as an indication of the reasons for the value decision—particularly important for cases in which the search is judged to be of little or no value. The user should also be asked to indicate how many items retrieved were useful in contributing to satisfying his information need (i.e., pertinent items). A distinction should be made between major value and lesser value items, perhaps along these lines:

1. Very important. I would not want to have missed these.
2. Pertinent to my interests but not so important.
3. Pertinent but of marginal value. The search would not have suffered much if these had not been retrieved.

It might also be useful to find out how many of the pertinent items are *new* to the user (i.e., items brought to his attention for the first time by the search) and to have the user give some blanket statement on why some other items retrieved were not pertinent to his interests. Finally, the user could be asked to give bibliographic data on items he felt should have been retrieved, because known to be pertinent, but were not. An evaluation form along the lines of Exhibit 32 might be suitable.

Based on data supplied on the evaluation form, the library can calculate a precision ratio for the search and also a cost per pertinent item retrieved. These figures can be based on items of any degree of pertinence or only on those judged more important (e.g., cost per "very important" item retrieved). It would also be possible to derive a *novelty ratio* for the search, i.e., the number of new and pertinent items retrieved

Search Evaluation

The printout attached presents the results of the search recently undertaken for you on the subject of _____ .

To help us monitor and improve our services would you please study the search results and answer the following questions:

1. Would you judge this search to be:

    Of great value _____   Of value _____
    Of little value _____   Of no value _____

2. Give a brief statement to explain the reason for your value judgment.

3. The search retrieved a total of _____ items. Please indicate how many were useful in contributing to the satisfaction of your information need according to scale presented below. (NOTE: In judging the importance of an item do *not* take into consideration whether or not you were previously familiar with it. Indicate how many items you were previously familiar with in the final column.)

	Number of items	Number previously familiar to you
A. These items are very important to me. The value of the search would have been greatly reduced had these been missed.	_____	_____
B. These are pertinent to my interests but of lesser importance. Nevertheless, it is good that they were retrieved.	_____	_____
C. These are pertinent but of very marginal value. The search would have been just as valuable without them.	_____	_____
D. These are not at all pertinent to my interests.	_____	_____

4. For the items judged D above please give some explanation as to why they were not pertinent:

5. If you are aware of any pertinent items that were not retrieved in this search, but probably should have been, please give bibliographic details below:

*   *   *   *   *   *   *

Exhibit 32

Draft of a search evaluation questionnaire

over the number of pertinent items retrieved, which would be especially useful in evaluating a search performed for current awareness purposes.

These performance figures can be used to monitor the service and to observe if its quality appears to improve over time (e.g., as the searchers gain more experience or after some change has been made in the service, such as adopting a new form to record the user's request). They must be used with considerable caution, however, because they do not provide a complete picture of the results of a search: the number of pertinent items missed is not known.

To obtain an estimated recall ratio requires considerable effort (and some cost) and a librarian will not want to go to this trouble for all searches performed. On the other hand, he should be willing to estimate recall for a sample of searches in order to get a more complete picture of the quality of this service. There are two practical ways in which the recall of a literature search can be estimated.

The first method involves the conduct of "parallel" searches by other members of the library staff. Suppose, for example, that the library employs three librarians who conduct searches for users. The "real" search for a particular user, performed by searcher A, retrieves a total of 40 references, of which 18 are judged pertinent by the user (precision is .45). Searcher B is asked to perform the same search. He is given the search statement of the user but not allowed to see the search strategy used by A. Presumably B may have a slightly different search approach and will thus retrieve a somewhat different set of references. Any items retrieved by B but not by A must be submitted to the requester of the search to be judged on the same scale of pertinence as before. If searcher B finds two pertinent items not found by A, A's recall can be estimated at 18/20 (i.e., $A/(A+B)$), or .9. The process can be repeated with searcher C. In this case the recall estimate would be based on $A/(A+B+C)$. If A's recall is to be based on the additional pertinent items found by B and C, the two sets of results (B or C items not found by A) should be combined for submission to the requester. Moreover, the parallel searches by B and C should not be held up pending receipt of the user's evaluation form, otherwise the later searches might be conducted after the data base has been updated by several thousand items, greatly complicating the comparisons. For this reason it might be desirable to establish in advance that the user is willing to cooperate in the evaluation.

The estimate of recall established in this way is really an upper bound value. For example if $A/(A+B+C)$ gives a value of 18/21, A's search could not have achieved better recall than 18/21, and the true recall may be somewhat less than this (A, B, and C combined might not have found *all* pertinent items, perhaps because of indexing errors). Nevertheless, for most purposes, the method will give perfectly acceptable results.

The second method of estimating recall is easier than the first although it is more difficult to explain clearly. Consider again the hypothetical search that retrieved 40 references, of which 18 are judged pertinent by the requester. Suppose the search falls in the field of electronics and has been performed in the INSPEC data base. It would be possible to do a second search in another data base that also covers electronics, such as COMPENDEX.* Let us say that the second search (which need not be comprehensive since it is the original search, not the second, that is being evaluated) retrieves 12 pertinent items. This set of 12 items can be used as a *sample* of pertinent items by which to estimate the recall of the original search. First, the 12 items must be compared against the 40 originally retrieved to see how many are duplicated in the two searches. This comparison may show that, of the 12, 10 were retrieved in the original search (8 judged pertinent and 2 not pertinent), leaving 2 about which nothing is known. Suppose that both of these new items are judged pertinent by the user. It must now be established that they appear in the INSPEC data base—e.g., by performing author searches. If they do, the estimated recall for the INSPEC search is 8/10, or .8. That is, of the *sample* of pertinent items found in the COMPEN-DEX data base (and also known to be in INSPEC), 8/10 were retrieved by the original search in INSPEC. Another way of looking at this result is that the 18 pertinent items retrieved in the INSPEC search are estimated to represent about 80% of the total of pertinent items in the INSPEC data base. This second method of estimating recall is likely to give a more accurate result than the first: if certain pertinent items have not been adequately indexed in the first data base they may not be retrieved however many people search for them but they might very well be exposed by a search in a second data base.

Improving the Service

Establishing performance results for a sample of searches (whether these results be recall ratios, precision ratios, cost per pertinent item, or whatever) does not in itself tell the librarian how the service might be improved. If one is serious about achieving improvement, one must undertake some analysis of reasons why failures occur in searches. Examples of *precision failures* (items retrieved that the user judged not

---

*For this purpose the equivalent printed tool, in this case the *Engineering Index*, might be used in place of an online search.

to be pertinent) can be identified from the search evaluation form. Why were such items retrieved? The most likely explanation will be one of the following:

1. The searcher did not clearly understand what the user wanted.
2. The search was performed more broadly than it should have been.
3. The vocabulary of the data base (e.g., thesaurus terms) was not specific enough to allow this search to be conducted with high precision.
4. Errors of indexing occur in the data base.

Examples of *recall failures* can be identified through the procedures used to arrive at the recall estimates. Recall failures will usually be due to one of these causes:

The searcher did not clearly understand what the user wanted.
The searcher did not explore all reasonable search approaches.
The structure of the vocabulary (e.g., thesaurus) did not give the searcher enough help in identifying appropriate terms.
Errors of indexing occur in the data base.

It is clear that some factors affecting the performance of a literature searching service in a particular library are outside the control of the library itself (i.e., under the control only of the data base producer or, possibly, the computer center making the data base accessible). Nevertheless, the librarian can use evaluation procedures to identify problems that *are* under local control and can be corrected—perhaps by further training in search techniques or by changing the procedures by which the library staff determine the needs of users (e.g., improved interviewing methods or a redesigned form for capturing the user's request statement).

Subject Searches in the Catalog of a Library

It should be noted that the criteria and procedures used to evaluate a subject search in an online data base would be equally applicable to the evaluation of a subject search in a printed index. With some modifications they would also apply to the evaluation of subject searching in a card catalog.

The efficiency of such a search can be expressed in terms of the cost *in time* per pertinent item found. Thus, if a user spends 15 minutes at the catalog to find three books he wishes to consult or borrow, the cost per item is 5 minutes of the user's time. An equivalent of the precision ratio could also be applied to this situation, but it would be a rather artificial measure based on the number of cards the user must examine to find the three items he judges pertinent. A recall ratio could be established by having searches on the user's topic performed by experienced librarians, but this measure would only be meaningful for the (probably rare) case in which the user wants to find everything the library owns on some topic. More sensible perhaps would be to use the experienced librarians to determine whether or not the user found the books that seem to be "best" (e.g., those that contain the most information, are most up-to-date, or emanate from the most authoritative sources).

In evaluating a subject search in an online catalog, the performance criteria would be (a) cost, in time, per pertinent item found (or, less desirable, number of entries examined and number judged pertinent), and (b) some estimate of recall or, better, a determination of whether or not the best items were found. Pertinent items overlooked by the user can be identified by searches performed by experienced librarians.

Study Questions

1. The research department of a small pharmaceutical company employs 25 research scientists and one technical information specialist. The company is very information-conscious and much of the time of the information specialist is spent in searching online data bases to provide references needed to support the work of the researchers. In fact, it has reached the point at which the demand for searches is beginning to exceed the capacity of the information specialist. He requests that a second information specialist be appointed. The Director of Research thinks he has a better idea. Since terminals are readily available throughout the department, he proposes that the information specialist, in conjunction with some outside information consultants, should train each of the 25 scientists in the techniques of online searching. Once trained, the scientists will do their own searches directly. The information specialist argues that this is undesirable from the viewpoint of effectiveness (*he* is better at searching than the scientists will ever be) and cost-effectiveness (his salary is approximately half the average salary paid to the research scientists). The Director of Research, however, is convinced that, once trained, scientists can satisfy their own information needs more effectively by searching directly. He asks an

outside consultant to conduct an objective evaluation that will prove or disprove his point. You are the consultant. How will you do the study?

2. The searching of data bases has been increasing rapidly throughout the departmental libraries of a large university. The University Librarian is pleased with this. Nevertheless, she has a doubt: with the large number of data bases now accessible, how can one be sure that a librarian selects the "best" data base for any particular information need? How could you evaluate the present data base selection among the departmental libraries?

12. Resource Sharing

Libraries cooperate with each other by sharing resources in a variety of ways. Interlibrary lending is the most obvious example but other cooperative programs are also possible, including those for the acquisition of materials, for the storage of less used materials, for the support of regional reference libraries, and so on. Libraries share resources in order to improve their cost-effectiveness. This is demonstrated in Exhibit 33. A library may be able to satisfy 80 to 90% of the needs of users from its own resources. It cannot go much beyond this point economically because it would require a completely disproportionate expenditure to do so. For example, a library may be able to satisfy 90% of the needs for periodical articles by subscribing to 200 titles; to satisfy 95% may require 700 titles, and 98% satisfaction may entail use of as many as 2,000. A similar pattern of diminishing returns affects other services provided by libraries.

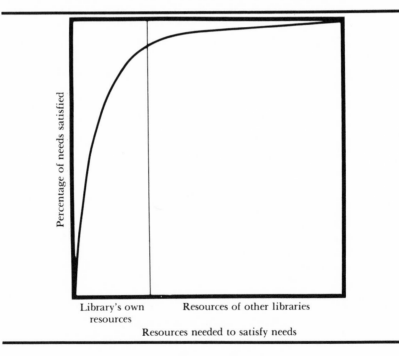

Exhibit 33
Cost-effectiveness justification for sharing of resources

Because library cooperation is now in such an advanced state in much of the developed world, a librarian can reasonably assume that almost any item can be acquired from another library if needed by a user. The decision on whether or not to purchase a particular item, then, is governed by the expected volume of use of the item and its cost. This can be seen most clearly in the case of a subscription to a periodical (Williams et al., 1968): for a title costing $50 per year, a level of demand as low as four uses a year may make it more economical to own the item than to acquire photocopies or tearsheets when user needs arise. For a title costing $500, of course, the level of demand would need to be very much greater to justify an annual subscription.*

The growth of electronic publishing over the last twenty years, together with the development of telecommunications networks to allow access to remote information sources, means that the tradeoff factors suggested by Exhibit 33 can be extended beyond the conventional concepts of "resource sharing." That is, acquisitions decisions now involve two general alternatives:

1. To make a capital investment in the ownership of a particular item and a continuing investment (e.g., in handling, storage) to keep it on the shelves. This can be considered as an investment in "access"—a book or other item is purchased in order to make it readily accessible to users.
2. To acquire access to the item, or part of it, as and when the need arises. This access could be achieved by borrowing, acquiring a photocopy/tearsheet/reprint, or (for some publications) accessing the item online.

To carry this to its logical conclusion, one could say that the *primary* collection of any library consists of those items that will be used so many times that they are worth buying outright, while the *secondary* collection is every other information resource, in whatever form, that can be acquired or accessed when needed. The corollary to this, of course, is that the "materials budget" of a library should become instead an "access budget" and that a librarian should be given a free hand to decide whether an item should be owned or access made available in some other way.**

---

*See King (1979) for a concise analysis of the buy versus borrow situation. The discussion in this paragraph is simplistic in that it fails to take copyright restrictions into consideration.

**I am greatly indebted to T.C. Dobb, University Librarian, Simon Fraser University, for the ideas encapsulated in this paragraph.

Evaluation Criteria

Many studies of the costs and of the effectiveness of resource sharing activities, especially interlibrary lending, have been carried out, although few true cost-effectiveness analyses have been performed. The criteria for evaluating the effectiveness of these activities seem fairly straightforward. For interlibrary loan the obvious criterion is fill rate or, more precisely, the number of items supplied in time to be of use to the requester (Cronin, 1985). Some procedures for collecting such data are given by Zweizig and Rodger (1982).

Possible criteria for the evaluation of various resource sharing activities can be found in a report by Peat, Marwick, Mitchell & Co. (1975). For interlibrary loan they advocate the collection of data on fill rate, delivery speed, transactions per request (i.e., the number of sources approached before a deliverable item is located), labor hours per request, and total cost per request. For cooperative reference services, data should be sought on the proportion of referred questions that are answered completely and correctly, on elapsed time, and on cost per question. Throughput time and cost per item are the obvious criteria to use in the evaluation of programs designed for cooperative cataloging and other types of cooperative processing.

Tools designed to facilitate resource sharing must be evaluated in terms of their effects on resource sharing activities. For example, the cost of building and maintaining an online union catalog must be balanced against the effect this tool has on fill rate, response time, and cost per transaction. A more subtle criterion is the contribution that the union catalog might make toward achieving a more equitable distribution of demand over participating libraries—insuring that the largest library in the system is the "source of last resort" rather than the source that all libraries automatically turn to.

To evaluate the success of some resource sharing activities, of course, the criteria will be less direct, and perhaps less obvious. One example is a program for coordinated collection building among a group of libraries. If such a program works effectively, the group presumably will be able to satisfy more demands from group resources than was possible before the program existed. At the same time, use per item purchased should increase and cost per use decline within the group as a whole. It is clear, then, that the true effects of resource sharing can only be determined when reliable quantitative and qualitative data exist to describe the situation before the resource sharing activity was initiated. Unfortunately, good "before" and "after" data rarely exist.

Many of the techniques described elsewhere in this book are as applicable to the resource sharing situation as they are to individual libraries. For example, the collection of a network of libraries can be evaluated by the methods discussed in Chapters 2-3 and availability rate within the network by the procedures described in Chapter 8. Studies of network resources are easily accomplished if the network makes use of a combined catalog/circulation system capable of showing the circulation status of any item owned by member libraries. Mansbridge (1984) has undertaken one of the few studies of availability within a network. The availability of items in the network to a particular library and the availability to the network of items in a particular library were both considered.

In the long run, resource sharing activities must be evaluated in terms of the extent to which they increase the effectiveness of library services or reduce the cost of providing an effective service. Cost-effectiveness is discussed in the next chapter.

Study Questions

1. A legislative committee has questioned the value of state support to cooperative library "systems" in Illinois. The committee wants an in-depth evaluation performed on one of the systems, the objective being to show that the funds expended are justified, either (a) in terms of greatly improved library and information services to the community or (b) in actual savings to the participating libraries. How would you perform such a study?

2. Two adjacent towns, serving populations of 35,000 and 65,000, have independent school systems. The education authorities in these communities believe that greater cooperation in educational activities would be mutually beneficial. You have been employed as a consultant to advise them on what types of cooperation might be possible in the area of school library services. What would you advise?

13. Cost-Effectiveness Considerations*

The term "cost-effectiveness" implies a relationship between the cost of providing some service and the level of effectiveness of that service. Throughout this book, *effectiveness* has been considered in terms of objective measures of success in satisfying user needs—proportion of factual questions answered completely and correctly, proportion of sought items immediately available to users, and so on. The cost-effectiveness of an operation can be improved by holding the level of effectiveness constant while reducing the cost of providing the service or by improving the effectiveness while holding costs constant. For example, it might be determined that the reference department of a public library is able to answer correctly 80% of the questions put to it. If it were possible to reduce costs of this service (perhaps by discontinuing subscriptions to some reference sources that are infrequently used), without affecting success in answering questions, the cost-effectiveness of the service would be improved. Of course, some service might be so inefficient that it would be possible to increase effectiveness while reducing costs, but this type of situation is rather rare.

Cost-effectiveness analyses can be thought of as studies of the costs associated with alternative strategies for achieving a particular level of effectiveness. To take a very simple example, suppose that the parents of two young children decide to buy an encyclopedia to help them with homework. A test with a few sample questions suggests that any one of three encyclopedias would be equally effective. If one of the encyclopedias costs less than the others, it can be considered the most "cost-effective" purchase.

It is relatively easy to think in terms of the cost-effectiveness of a single service but much more difficult to do so at an institutional level. Here, cost-effectiveness has to do with the optimum allocation of resources. Unfortunately, the different services provided by a library are competing with each other for limited funds. Moreover, effectiveness measures differ from service to service. If more resources are put into answering factual questions, the diversion of resources from elsewhere may reduce the effectiveness of other services. If success in question-answering goes

---

*Various aspects of cost-effectiveness have been discussed throughout the book. The present chapter tries to pull these together.

from 80 to 85%, but that in document delivery declines from 60 to 55%, it would be difficult for the librarian to claim that the reallocation of resources has improved the effectiveness of the institution. In a theoretically ideal situation, the allocation of resources would be so perfect that no amount of reallocation would improve the library's services to users. However, it is highly unlikely that such an ideal would ever be reached. Moreover, the existence of competing services, to which different effectiveness measures apply, would make it impossible to determine that the ideal had been achieved.

Cost Factors

Methods for establishing the costs of library operations have already been described in the literature (see, for example, Roberts, 1984; Citron and Dodd, 1984; Rosenberg, 1985) and need not be repeated here.* On the other hand, it does seem appropriate to reemphasize some of the points regarding costs that were made in Chapter 1.

In the performance of cost-effectiveness studies it is important that all appropriate costs be taken into account. The danger exists that less obvious costs may be overlooked. Two examples serve to illustrate the point:

1. In comparing the cost of performing searches in a printed tool, such as *Chemical Abstracts*, with that of performing searches in the online equivalent, the cost of owning the printed tool must be accounted for. A major element in the cost of an online search will be the cost of *access* to the data base (including computer costs, telecommunications costs, and data base royalties). The equivalent cost of access to the printed tool is the cost of the subscription, the cost of handling it (checking it in and so on), and the cost of the space it occupies. Thus, if it costs $5,000 a year to own a particular data base in printed form, and the data base is used 500 times each year, the cost of performing a search in this tool must include $10 for "access cost." Not to do so would give a completely distorted picture in the comparison of "manual" versus online searching (Elchesen, 1978; Lancaster, 1981).
2. Consider a comparison, within a particular company, of the cost of online searches performed by librarians with the cost of searches performed by company scientists on their own behalf. Suppose that, on the average, it costs $80 per hour to interrogate the data bases used

---

*Getz (1980), an economist, has accused librarians of ignoring costs in their evaluative studies. He, on the other hand, ignores effectiveness except in terms of circulation and other quantitative measures of use.

by the company (all costs except personnel costs) and that, on the average, a librarian spends 15 minutes online per search while the scientist spends 20 minutes. The librarian costs the company $20 per hour, while the scientist costs $30 per hour. Taking these factors into account, then, the average cost of a scientist search will be about $37 while the average cost of a search by the librarian will be $25. This comparison has overlooked the costs associated with the delegation of the search by scientist to librarian. For a scientist to describe an information need to a librarian may consume 15 minutes of the time of each party. Thus, for the delegated search situation one must add a further $7.50 in scientist time and $5.00 in librarian time, bringing the cost up to $37.50. Even this analysis is incomplete. If one assumes that the librarians have already been trained in online searching, but the scientists have not, it will be necessary to build into the calculations the cost of training the scientists—and this cost must be amortized over some period of time.

These figures are purely hypothetical and certain assumptions underlie the analysis (e.g., that all scientists have suitable terminals in their offices). The whole situation has been deliberately oversimplified in order to illustrate what can happen when significant costs are overlooked. A more sophisticated analysis would need to take into account how librarians and scientists would spend their time if they were not online to data bases.

Cost-effectiveness Measures

A cost-effectiveness study looks at return on investment. As implied earlier, the "return" on a library's investment (in material, personnel, and facilities) can be measured in service to users. More precisely, a good cost-effectiveness measure is one that balances cost against some unit of user satisfaction. The literature searching situation provides a good example. As discussed in Chapter 11, the success of a bibliographic search can be expressed in terms of the number of pertinent items retrieved. An appropriate cost-effectiveness measure, then, is the cost per pertinent item retrieved. Returning to an example used earlier, one could compare online searching by librarians with searching by scientists on the basis of (a) cost, (b) effectiveness, or (c) cost-effectiveness. Consider the following data:

	Librarian	Scientist
Cost	$37 per search	$40 per search
Effectiveness	15 pertinent items retrieved on the average	20 pertinent items retrieved on the average
Cost-Effectiveness	$2.47 per pertinent item retrieved	$2 per pertinent item retrieved

The cost comparison favors the librarian, but the effectiveness and cost-effectiveness comparisons both favor the scientist. A more sophisticated analysis would distinguish between "major value" and "minor value" items; e.g., the scientist might find more than the librarian but the librarian finds the ones that the scientist judges most valuable, perhaps because it is these that are "new" to him.

The literature searching situation is unusual in that the cost-effectiveness measure seems relatively clearcut and easily defended. For other components of library service, it may be less clear what the best measure of cost-effectiveness should be. Take the case of a subscription to a periodical. One possible measure of return on investment would be the number of articles it publishes annually that are likely to be of direct interest to the library's users. This is more obviously appropriate in the case of a highly specialized library. For example, based on past performance, journal A can be expected to publish about twelve "irrigation" articles each year, while journal B can be expected to publish about twenty. A costs \$120 to subscribe to while B costs \$250. In return on investment, A is a somewhat better buy for an irrigation library, always assuming that an article in A is "as good" as one in B. In the case of a more general library, however, such a measure of "yield" seems much less appropriate and would be exceedingly difficult to apply.

The most obvious measure of return on investment for an item purchased is the number of uses it receives. In a very superficial sense, a book that costs \$75 to acquire and make ready for the shelves is a more cost-effective purchase, if used 20 times in its lifetime in the library, than one that costs \$30 and receives six uses. The problem with this, of course, is that all uses are presumed "equal," which many librarians are quite unwilling to accept. If cost per use were the only consideration, a public library could improve its overall cost-effectiveness by buying more and more of the highly popular items at the expense of materials in categories of lower demand. Such a strategy is sometimes advocated (see, for example, Newhouse and Alexander, 1972) although it completely ignores the need to build a "balanced" collection and to serve the needs of a wide variety of users, some of whom might be quite atypical of the majority. In an academic library, of course, amount of use is even less acceptable as a measure of success in book selection (see Voigt, 1979, for example); indeed, some university librarians seem to place more value on potential use than they do on actual use.

Nevertheless, cost per use cannot be dismissed entirely. As Kent et al. (1979) have shown, the cost-effectiveness of a collection of periodicals can drop dramatically when titles receiving no use at all are retained in the collection. Cost per use or expected use will be an obvious criterion governing many decisions—whether to subscribe to a new periodical, whether to discontinue some publication for which an online equivalent exists, whether to purchase some expensive reference tool, and so on.

Since the space occupied by a library is not "free," one type of cost-effectiveness analysis has to do with the optimum use of space, especially the space occupied by materials. Some aspects of this were discussed in Chapter 6. As suggested there, use per unit of shelf space occupied is a criterion that should be considered in deciding which materials to dispose of or to relegate to less accessible storage areas.

Diminishing Returns

The phenomenon of diminishing returns is of great importance when the cost-effectiveness of any operation is taken into account. Many manifestations exist. One, mentioned earlier, relates to the special library situation in which the cost of subscribing to periodicals is balanced against their potential yield of papers directly related to the scope of the library.

If the journal titles contributing papers on a particular subject are arranged in descending order of their yield, the familiar "scatter" phenomenon (Bradford, 1948) will be observed: a small number of journals (the "core" or "nucleus") will contribute a disproportionately large number of papers, but much of the literature will be widely scattered over very many titles. Exhibit 34 shows some hypothetical data covering a period of, say, three years. The journal at the top of the list has contributed 314 papers on the subject in this period, the second has contributed a further 265 papers, and so on down to 130 journals that have published only one paper each on the subject in three years. In all, 252 journals are needed to contribute all 1757 papers on the subject, but almost one-third of the papers appear in the first two journals only.

Besides the scatter data, Exhibit 34 presents subscription costs associated with each line of the table. It costs almost $12,000 to acquire all 252 journals but about a third of the literature can be obtained by subscribing to only the first two on the list, which will cost $525.

Exhibit 35 presents the data in graphical form. One-third of the periodical literature can be acquired at subscription costs of $525 but it would cost about three times this much to acquire two-thirds. The law of diminishing returns is demonstrated with a vengeance after about the 80% level. It costs more to go from 80% to 90% than it does to go from 0 to 80%.

The data of Exhibit 34 suggest several possible selection strategies. For example, it might be decided to subscribe only to titles that yield 7 or

Journals	Articles	Cumulation Journals	Cumulation Articles	Cost ($) (cumulative)
1	314	1	314	450
1	265	2	579	525
1	223	3	802	550
1	48	4	850	785
2	37	6	924	809
1	29	7	953	874
1	23	8	976	902
1	22	9	998	916
1	21	10	1019	964
2	19	12	1057	994
1	17	13	1074	1271
2	15	15	1104	1431
2	14	17	1132	1451
4	13	21	1184	1479
2	12	23	1208	1503
1	11	24	1219	1516
2	10	26	1239	1576
7	9	33	1302	1629
5	8	38	1342	1829
2	7	40	1356	1869
8	6	48	1404	2245
11	5	59	1459	2762
12	4	71	1507	3326
18	3	89	1561	4172
33	2	122	1627	5723
130	1	252	1757	11833

Exhibit 34

Periodical titles ranked by decreasing yield of articles on
some specialized topic over a 3-year period

more papers per year. If this were so, the top 10 journals on the list
would be purchased at an annual cost of $964. The top 10 journals can
be expected to yield about 55% of the relevant articles. If the cutoff was
put at 5 papers per year, the number of journals goes up to 15 and the
subscription cost to $1431. This would yield about 63% of the relevant
articles.

Another possible strategy would be to leave out the more expensive
medium-yield journals. For example, the journal ranked 13 costs $277 a
year yet yields only about 6 articles per year. If this title were omitted, the
top 15 titles would yield 1101 papers (about 63% of the total) at a
subscription cost of only $1,164. This would probably be the preferred
strategy if the library had only about $1,200 to spend or if cost per article
is the criterion governing the decision.

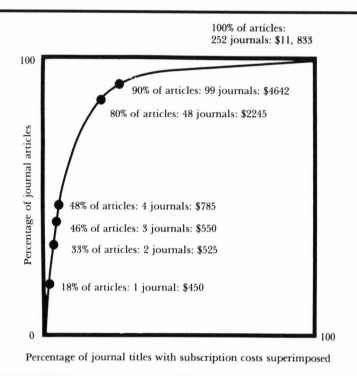

100% of articles:
252 journals: $11, 833

90% of articles: 99 journals: $4642

80% of articles: 48 journals: $2245

48% of articles: 4 journals: $785

46% of articles: 3 journals: $550

33% of articles: 2 journals: $525

18% of articles: 1 journal: $450

Percentage of journal articles

Percentage of journal titles with subscription costs superimposed

Exhibit 35
Yield versus subscription costs

It is obvious that a special library trying to build a strong collection in this subject area can only acquire about 60-70% of the periodical literature by direct subscription. Not only would it be uneconomical to try for much more, it would be virtually impossible: as one goes down the table (Exhibit 34), the predictability declines rapidly with the decreasing yield. That is, the most productive journals for this subject are likely to be the most productive for some time to come, whereas the 130 journals at the bottom of the list, which have only contributed one paper each in the last three years, may never contribute again. As one proceeds down past the middle of the table, one is less and less confident that a journal contributing a few papers each year will continue to do so. For the 30-40% of the periodical literature that cannot be acquired by direct subscription, this special library must turn to secondary sources—

Current Contents, printed indexing/abstracting services, or regular searches in online data bases.

This discussion of the special library problem has been a little oversimplified in that it takes into consideration only the subject matter central to the library's interests. The data might relate, say, to the subject of agricultural communications. A library devoted to this subject will collect materials in related areas, including agriculture in general and communications technology. Looked at in this broader context, somewhat different subscription decisions might be made. For example, some journals yielding only 3 or 4 papers per year on agricultural communications might still be wanted if these are key journals in the broader fields.

A ranked list of the journals contributing articles on some subject, such as Exhibit 34, can be valuable in a number of ways. Having such a list can bring to the attention of a librarian high-yielding journals that may have been overlooked including, perhaps, some inexpensive journals that might add significantly to coverage at little extra cost.

Hyperbolic curves of the type shown in Exhibit 35 completely typify the phenomenon of diminishing returns. The phenomenon was encountered in earlier chapters. Most obviously, the curve is similar to that derived when the number of volumes in a collection is plotted against the number of circulations (see Exhibit 6). In fact, the 80/20 rule applies well to these scatter data: 80% of the papers come from 19% of the journals.

Another example of diminishing returns has been presented by Powell (1976). In studying the size of reference collections in Illinois public libraries, Powell discovered (Exhibit 36) that a collection of around 3,000 volumes seemed about "optimum." A collection of this size might answer 90% or so of a selected group of questions. To raise this to 95% might entail a leap to as many as 12,000 volumes. Exhibit 36 illustrates once more the phenomenon of unpredictability. It is possible that a very large proportion—perhaps 70%—of questions received by a small public library could be answered by as few as 20 or 30 well selected tools—one encyclopedia, one dictionary, an almanac, local directories, two or three major biographical sources, a book of quotations, and so on. This is because many of the questions received are of the same general type and quite predictable. After, say, the 70% level, the predictability greatly declines. One might need several hundred volumes to answer 80% of the questions and several thousand to answer 90%. Exhibit 36 provides a dramatic demonstration of the advantages of resource sharing. A public library might need many thousands of volumes to answer 90-95% of the questions it receives in a year but it might be able to answer 80% with a small fraction of these. From a cost-effectiveness point of view, it would make sense for each public library to lower its sights—to aim to answer, say, 80% of the questions from its own resources but to have ready access by telephone or online network to a regional or statewide reference library designed to answer the more obscure and less predictable questions.*

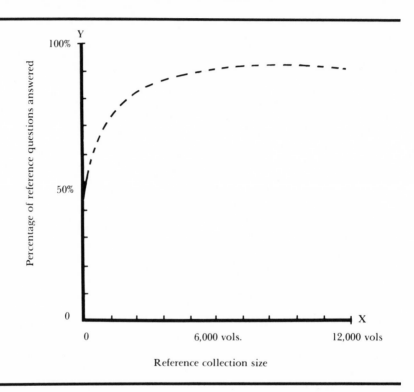

Exhibit 36

Relationship between the size of a reference collection and the percentage of test questions that a library can answer correctly. Adapted from Benham and Powell (1987) by permission of Scarecrow Press Inc.

---

*From a cost-effectiveness point of view it makes little sense for an individual library to attempt to satisfy more than some specified percentage of total demands (of any type) from its own resources. It is this fact that justifies resource sharing and makes such activities central to library service. In this the author differs from those librarians (e.g., Ballard, 1985, 1986) who regard resource sharing as a peripheral activity, or even one that is unjustified.

The 90 Percent Library

The law of diminishing returns leads naturally to the idea of the 90% library. The idea (Bourne, 1965) is simply this: it is possible for a library service to satisfy some large proportion—say 90%—of all demands efficiently and economically, but it would take a completely disproportionate amount of money and/or effort to raise this by as little as another 2 or 3%. This is due to the unpredictability problem mentioned earlier. Some examples of the phenomenon, several of which have already been mentioned, are as follows:

1. Ninety percent of the factual questions received might be answered from 3,000 volumes. Ninety-five percent may require an increase to 12,000 volumes.
2. Ninety percent of the periodical articles requested by users of a special library may come from 80 periodical titles. To raise this to 95% may require an increase to 300 titles.
3. Ninety percent of the circulations in a public library may come from 20% of the collection but 95% of the circulations are accounted for by 60% of the collection.
4. Ninety percent of the demands for periodical articles may be satisfied by journal issues no more than five years old. To satisfy 95% of the demands may require that one go back 50 years (Exhibit 37).

A generalized representation of the 90% library phenomenon is presented in Exhibit 38, which shows that, in terms of satisfying user needs (for documents, for answers to questions, or whatever), the resources needed to go from 90% satisfaction to 95% may exceed the resources needed to go from 0 to 90%. The greater the success rate demanded, the more disproportionate becomes the required expenditure of resources. Librarians must recognize the fact that one can satisfy all of the users some of the time, or some of the users all of the time, but not all of the users all of the time.

Some writers in library science fail to distinguish clearly between cost-effectiveness and cost-benefit studies.* The latter, quite different from the former, are dealt with in the next chapter.

---

*For example, Schauer (1986), while he points out that a cost-benefit study is not the same as a cost-effectiveness study, fails to distinguish clearly between the two.

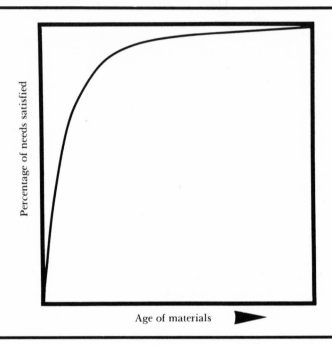

Exhibit 37
Decline in use with age

Study Questions

1. You are the Undergraduate Librarian in a large university. A new periodical on popular science has been brought to your attention. It is within scope and will cost $80 a year to subscribe to. You know that another periodical on popular science, also costing $80, is so heavily used that it is rarely available when sought by users. How will you decide on whether to spend the $80 on the new title or on a second copy of the heavily used one?

2. A small college library has been holding on to its subscription to *Chemical Abstracts* despite substantial increases in costs. Although chemistry is part of the curriculum, a new librarian is reluctant to

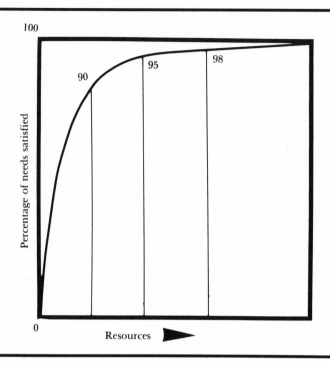

Exhibit 38
Generalized representation of the 90% library phenomenon

maintain the subscription any longer, preferring to pay for access to the data base online when necessary. What data should he collect in order to be able to justify his decision on cost-effectiveness grounds?

3. The National Institutes of Health is establishing a new information center on the subject of Acquired Immune Deficiency Syndrome (AIDS). You are the first librarian. You have $8,000 to spend on periodical subscriptions. How will you decide which periodicals to acquire in order to get the best return on your investment?

14. Cost-Benefit Studies

Although the terminology is used rather loosely, a cost-benefit analysis is quite different from a cost-effectiveness study. "Cost-benefit," clearly, refers to a relationship between the cost of some activity and the benefits derived from it. In effect, a cost-benefit study is one that tries to justify the existence of the activity by demonstrating that the benefits outweigh the costs. Ideally, the benefits should be expressed in the same units of measurement as the costs, that is in $, £, or some other currency. Unfortunately it is exceptionally difficult, if not completely impossible, to express the benefits of library service in monetary units. Indeed, it is not easy to think of the benefits derived from a library in any but subjective terms.

As suggested in Chapter 1, the benefits of a library relate to outcomes or impact. In a sense, the very existence of a library in a community or institution implies that some individuals at some time made the decision that the cost of supporting the library is justified by the expected benefits.

It may be possible to look at impact of an information service at various levels, as follows:

1. Existence
2. Awareness
3. Trial
4. Adoption
5. Referral
6. True impact or benefit

These six levels of impact, which are not unlike the stages usually associated with the diffusion of innovation (Rogers and Shoemaker, 1971), are presented in a sequence of increasing significance. They are best explained within the context of a particular type of information service, say an employment agency.

The first level, "existence," may be thought rather trivial. One might argue, however, that the mere establishment of the employment agency, where no such agency existed previously, must have some impact in and of itself, although it is not known how much the impact will be.

"Awareness" is a more significant measure of impact. It seems reasonable to suppose that the more people who are aware of the existence of the agency (determined through some type of survey) the greater its impact; it can hardly have much impact if no-one knows it exists.

One step beyond awareness is "trial." The potential impact of the agency increases with the number of employers and job seekers who make some use of its services. "Adoption" goes further. It implies that some companies are sufficiently satisfied with the service that they become regular customers. The more regular customers, the greater the impact.

The more satisfied the customers of the agency, the more likely they are to recommend its services to others. The number of referrals that occur can thus be considered another measure of impact. The true impact, however, has to do with the real objective of the agency, which is to match employers with job seekers. The agency benefits the community it serves to the extent that individuals can use its services to locate suitable jobs and companies to find suitable employees.

In theory, these levels of impact could be applied to, say, a public library. Its potential impact increases with the number of people in the community who are aware of its existence and of the services it provides. "Trial" can be expressed in terms of the number of individuals in the community who register for a library card and "adoption" in terms of the number who have used the library at least X times in the past year. Referral would be more difficult to measure.

The public library differs most from the employment agency in the final level of true impact. It is quite clear why the latter exists, what its objectives are, and in what terms its benefits should be expressed, but it is much less clear what the desired outcomes of the public library are.

Approaches to the Measurement of Benefits

In the cost-benefit context, industrial libraries differ somewhat from public, school, or academic libraries. On the one hand, it is more likely that librarians in industry will be asked to justify the library's existence in monetary terms. On the other hand, it is a little easier to think of the benefits of the library in the same terms—i.e., the extent to which the library contributes to the profit-making activities of the company. It is hardly surprising, then, that more attempts at cost-benefit analysis have been applied to industrial libraries than to libraries of other kinds.

Various approaches to measuring the benefits of an information service have been discussed or tried.* In order of increasing sophistication, these are:

1. Net value approach
2. Value of reducing uncertainty
3. Cost of buying service elsewhere
4. Librarian time replaces user time
5. Service improves organization's performance or saves the organization money:
    a) duplication avoided
    b) loss of productivity avoided
    c) cheaper solution suggested
    d) invention stimulated

The "net value" approach is extremely simplistic. The net value of an information service to a user is considered to be the maximum amount he is willing to pay (gross value) minus the actual cost. For example, suppose a small company asks an information broker to find a particular item of information—say to determine if data exist on the thermal conductivity of a particular alloy. The company gives the broker authority to spend up to $5,000 to locate the data (*gross value*), which implies that the data are worth at least this much to the company. In fact, the broker is able to find the data at a cost of $200. The *net value* of this service to the company is thus calculated as $4,800.

The value of information to an individual can often be thought of in terms of the extent to which it reduces his uncertainty. This is most clear in the situation in which the seeker of information could make a good decision or a bad decision especially, perhaps, if there are actual costs associated with these decisions. Consider, for example, a man who has decided to buy a particular model of video recorder. At the time this decision is made, three stores in his community carry the model and offer it at widely different prices:

Store	Cost ($)
A	225
B	282
C	214

Clearly, the best decision would be to go to store *C* and the worst would be to go to *B*. The *maximum potential benefit* to be derived from this

---

*A number of examples of these various approaches can be found in a report by Plate (1983).

information is $68, which is the difference between the most that could be paid and the least that could be paid ($282 - 214 = 68). Suppose that a data base exists that provides information on the current prices of products within local stores (offered perhaps by some videotex service), and that the consumer can obtain the information noted above at a cost of $12. The *net benefit* to the user of having this information can be considered to be $56 (the maximum potential benefit, $68, minus actual cost).*

Consumer information is perhaps the prime example of information to which a monetary value can frequently be given. Take a somewhat different example. A young woman wants to buy a particular kind of exercise machine. A consumer magazine has tested these machines and found three models to be equally acceptable. The models are priced at $327, $344, and $405. The maximum potential benefit of this information to the consumer in this case is $78. It might well be worth her while to visit the local public library to check the consumer ratings. For a less expensive purchase—say a toaster—similar ratings may be considered less important.

Some industrial librarians have attempted to justify the existence of their services by calculating how much it would cost the company to buy equivalent services from elsewhere—another library within the organization itself, an external library, or a commercial information service (see, for example, Magson, 1973). In this case, the underlying assumption is that the service is worthwhile. The question being considered is whether it is better for the company to provide the service through an in-house library or in some other way.** The entire range of services offered by the library can be considered in such a study. Alternatively, a single service can be the focus of attention. For example, it might be determined that the total cost of providing online literature searches through the library, at a level of 500 searches a year, is $35,000. To buy this level of service from a commercial agency might cost $50,000. Thus, the net benefit to the company of providing the service in-house is $15,000.

In many ways this is a reasonable approach to justifying the existence of a library of this type, although there are certain problems associated with it. Some services may not be suitable for delegation to an outside contractor for reasons of practicality or of industrial security.

---

*For a more complete discussion of this type of approach see Wills and Christopher (1970).

**One could argue perhaps that this is more a cost-effectiveness study comparing alternative strategies) than a cost-benefit study.

There might be a certain "convenience" factor associated with the in-house facility that the outside agency could not duplicate, although it would be difficult to give this factor any real monetary value. A more practical problem is the fact that the collection of materials owned by the library is likely to contribute to many different services—document delivery, literature searching, question answering, preparation of an information bulletin—and it is difficult to allocate the costs of the collection over the various services in any meaningful way. Nevertheless, if corporate management is satisfied with this approach to the justification of services, it has a lot to commend it from the librarian's point of view.

A somewhat similar approach compares the cost of the librarian providing some service with the cost of the librarian's customers undertaking the activity for themselves (Mason, 1972; Rosenberg, 1969). To take a very simple example, suppose that the average cost of a literature search provided by the librarian is $140 and it is calculated that the average cost of an equivalent search undertaken by a customer himself (e.g., a research scientist) would be $195, because of salary differential. It could be argued, then, that the librarian saves the company $55 for every search performed.

Of course, there are some underlying assumptions here: that the scientist would do the search if the librarian was not available and that the scientist's results would be qualitatively equivalent to those of the librarian.

Rosenberg (1969) tried to carry this method further by having users "weight" the results of a literature search performed by the librarian, according to the scale.

0 Useless (e.g., because not relevant or received too late).
1 Adequate. User would have spent same amount of time as librarian.
2 Good. User would have spent twice the amount of time spent by the librarian.
3 Excellent. Results could not have been achieved by user or could not have been achieved at an acceptable cost.

These weights may be built into a "savings" equation, $(A \times B \times C - A$, where A is the cost of the librarian's time, B a multiplication factor to account for the difference in salary between librarian and engineer, and C the assigned weighting factor. Thus, if a literature search costs $75 in librarian time, the salary differential is 1.5, and the weight given by the user is 2, the savings would be calculated as ($75 \times 1.5 \times 2$) - 75, or $150.

Clearly this is very subjective, for one can have little confidence that a user could arrive at any realistic estimate of how much time it would take to perform some information retrieval task. Several other investigators have tried to justify an information service by estimating potential cost savings attributable to having these services available. It is assumed that, were the library not available, engineers or scientists would spend more of their own time in information seeking and that this would be costly to the organization. Analyses of this type are only as good as the validity of the estimates of time saved.

Nightingale (1973) provides an example of one approach. He calculated that it cost £ 2500 per year to produce a company abstracts bulletin. By means of a survey, he determined how many journals were regularly scanned by the recipients of the bulletin and had them estimate how many additional journals they would want to scan for themselves if the bulletin was discontinued. A median value of 6 additional journals per user was obtained. Nightingale calculated that it would take a user 10 minutes, on the average, to scan a journal in order to identify items of interest. The cost of this activity was estimated at 18.5 hours per user per year (6 journals x 10 minutes x number of issues), which worked out to £ 74. With 400 users, the cost of the extra scanning would be £ 74 x 400, or £ 29,600. The bottom line of the cost benefit analysis, then, is a saving annually of £ 27,100 (£ 29,600 less the cost of producing the bulletin).

Nightingale's analysis seems reasonably conservative. Much less conservative are the data reported by Kramer (1971), based on a study performed at Boeing Aerospace. Kramer estimated savings to the company attributable to having the library perform literature searches and answer factual questions, as opposed to having the engineers do this for themselves. Questionnaires returned by 153 engineers, for whom literature searches had been performed, estimated that 9,479 hours of engineering time would have been consumed had the engineers conducted the searches themselves. The librarian time to perform these searches was calculated to be 1,071 manhours (about 7 per search). Clearly, even if the librarian is paid at the same rate as the engineer, the savings would seem to be considerable. About 8,000 hours of engineer time at 1987 rates (and including all overheads) might work out at over $300,000.

Kramer also used follow-up telephone interviews with 215 engineers for whom the library had answered factual questions. While the librarians averaged 12 minutes per question, the engineers estimated that it would have taken them an average of 5.42 hours per question to find the answer!! For 215 questions this represents another 1,166 manhours of engineering time saved.

Estabrook (1986) also asked engineers to estimate time savings associated with use of a search/document delivery service, and to put a dollar value on the information retrieved. She concluded that, by the most conservative estimates, the company saved two dollars for every one expended on the service. In best-case terms, however, the company might save almost $50 for each $1 invested in the information center. This latter information was arrived at by including two extreme cases in which the recipients of information estimated potential savings of $1 million and $2.5 million.

A number of other studies have also attempted to get users to place a dollar value on the results received from some information service. For example, Jensen et al. (1980) report that of 159 users of an online searching service surveyed, 53% were able to identify dollar benefits. These users reported "current benefits" of $364,605 and "5 year follow-on benefits" of $873,500.

Data of these kind would provide a very impressive endorsement of an information service if they were fully credible. Unfortunately, it is difficult to believe that anyone could come up with a realistic estimate of how long it would take to perform a particular information retrieval activity, and the results achieved by Kramer (almost 30 times longer for an engineer to answer a question than for the librarian) strain the bounds of credibility. It seems even less likely that the user of an information service can put a dollar value on information received with any degree of accuracy, although Estabrook (1986) claims that such estimates may be better than are commonly supposed.

Even if an exact dollar value cannot be placed upon a piece of information, there may be occasions when an industrial information service may prove its worth to the corporation in a dramatic way. In the case of a research organization, the greatest benefit that the library can provide might be the uncovering of information that prevents the company from performing research already done elsewhere. It is difficult to document events of this type (and even more difficult to prove that the company would not have found the information without the library) but a single case, if documented, might justify the cost of the library for several years. A large study of the unintentional duplication of research, and the cost of this duplication, was performed in the United Kingdom by Martyn (1964). Martyn presents impressive evidence to support the claim that large amounts of money could be saved by the performance of more complete literature searches before research projects get underway. M. Cooper (1968) presents figures on the saving of research time attributable to the informal communications distributed experimentally by the information exchange groups established by the National Institutes of Health.

Another possible measure of benefit is the loss of productivity that might occur if the library were not available in a company and the scientists or engineers were forced to wait much longer for needed information. Mueller (1959), for example, discovered that the work of some engineers was actually brought to a halt while waiting for information to complete a critical task. The assumption here, of course, is that having information saves time. Solomin (1974) has argued that, under certain circumstances, having information increases company costs because it requires the expenditure of time to process and assimilate it.

Finally, a librarian might point to other positive effects on the company that can be traced to information provided by the librarians. These might include the development of a new product, the identification of ways to reduce the costs of existing products (e.g., by use of materials that are cheaper but equally effective), or the award of an important contract. It is not easy to prove that the library has been directly responsible for events of this kind, but a single documented example might be sufficient to justify the library's existence for some time to come.

Investigators at King Research Inc. (1982) have carried cost-benefit analysis even further in trying to determine the value of the Energy Data Base (U.S. Department of Energy). Through use of questionnaires, it was estimated that the reading of articles and reports by DOE-funded scientists and engineers resulted in the location of information yielding annual savings of $13 billion (in avoiding duplication of work, saving time, and in other ways). This contrasts with an annual expenditure by DOE for research and development of $5.3 billion and an expenditure of $500 million on information processing and use.

In the opinion of this author, no completely credible or definitive cost-benefit studies have been applied to industrial libraries, and there seems even less prospect of performing such studies in academic, public, or school libraries whose objectives are inherently more nebulous.

Study Questions

1. The administrator of a hospital would like to save some money by closing the hospital library. As the librarian, what evidence would you collect to persuade the administrator that this would be a shortsighted act?

2. The Russell Chemical Company has not been doing well financially for the past three years. So far the library has escaped the axe. The Director of Research, to whom the Librarian reports, is very supportive of the library and wants to shield the service from possible future attack. He wants to gather data to prove that the library provides benefits to the company that far exceed the costs of providing the service. You are the Librarian and you have been asked to undertake this cost-benefit analysis as a top priority. What approaches would you use?

3. What are the benefits of a school library? How would you conduct a cost-benefit study in this environment?

15. Afterword

No attempt has been made in this volume to cover all aspects of the evaluation of library services or to include various subjects tangential to evaluation. A comprehensive treatment of this kind would result in a much larger book. In this final chapter some additional aspects of evaluation will at least be mentioned; where appropriate, reference will be made to sources of further information.

Technical Services

The focus of attention in preceding chapters has been the public services offered by libraries. Technical processes have been covered only to the extent that their outputs contribute to the effectiveness or cost-effectiveness of public services. The most obvious example is that of cataloging. It is not useful to consider the effectiveness of cataloging except in terms of the end result of the activity, the catalog itself. Similarly, book selection can only be evaluated meaningfully in terms of the end results of this activity, the collection.

Nevertheless, it is both possible and meaningful to evaluate the *efficiency* of technical services in and of themselves. Time and cost factors are paramount in evaluations of efficiency. For example, important considerations include how much it costs on the average to catalog a monograph, how much to prepare an item for the shelf, and the total cost of adding a monograph to the collection. Time factors to be considered are of two types: time expended and time elapsed. Time expended by staff members in the conduct of some activity, of course, may well be the major component in the cost of that activity. Elapsed time need not be directly related to costs but will still be an important element of efficiency. Most obvious is the time elapsing from the date a book arrives in a library to the date it is available for public use. Since the demand for most books is likely to be at its peak shortly after publication, it is important that these items reach the shelves as rapidly as possible.

Data needed to evaluate the efficiency of technical services can be collected in a number of ways such as direct observation and the application of various types of log, including use of random alarm devices. Use of logs (e.g., a daily log prepared by a staff member or a form that accompanies an item through a sequence of processes) is illustrated by

Martyn and Lancaster (1981), while examples of the use of random alarms can be found in Spencer (1971, 1974), and Divilbiss and Self (1978). Some novel techniques applicable to the evaluation of technical services are presented by Wessel (1968).

Range and Scope of Services

This topic was discussed in some detail in an earlier book (Lancaster, 1977). As described by Orr et al. (1968b), a standardized procedure can be applied to determine precisely what services are offered by a particular library and what policies affect use of these services. In Orr's work, and in an application to Indiana libraries described by Olson (1970), a quantitative score is derived to reflect the range and scope of the services offered by a library and to allow comparisons to be made among libraries.

Single Figure of Merit

The work of Orr and Olson on the range and scope of services leads eventually to the derivation of a numerical value on some scale—e.g., a library may score 750/1000. Other evaluators have tried to arrive at a meaningful "single figure of merit" for library services. For example, a working group of the (Canadian) Council of Federal Libraries (1979) proposed the following scoring method:

	Points or weight
Information delivery	100
Document delivery	100
Timely document delivery	85
Current awareness	70
Collections	40
Catalogs	25

for a total of 420 "points." If procedures are developed for evaluating a library on each of these services/tools, it would be possible to derive some composite score.

This type of index of effectiveness has obvious appeal: were it possible to achieve some consensus on point allocation and testing procedures, one would have a scoring method that could be applied to compare different libraries. Unfortunately, it is almost impossible to achieve such consensus among librarians. Moreover, even if a consensus were obtained, the single figure of merit obscures important data. For example, a library might do extremely well on document delivery but very badly on question answering. The single score, obviously, does not indicate such important differences. White (1977) gives a useful review of various approaches to arriving at a single figure of merit for libraries.

O'Connor (1982) has gone much further: he has developed "standard scores" for public libraries where a library's position on a particular scale is a function of the positions of all other libraries. However, the data used in O'Connor's scores are not the results of true evaluation activities but quantitative measures of input and output.

Library Standards

In the author's earlier book (Lancaster, 1977), the relevance of standards to the evaluation of library services was one topic discussed. It was pointed out that library standards are guidelines rather than the type of enforceable standard that operates within industry. They tend to be derived by looking at quantitative aspects of selected institutions that are considered to be "good" institutions. Such aspects would include size of collection, hours of service, space, seating, and so on. Library standards emphasize inputs (resources) rather than outputs (services). They have some value as procedural guidelines, in establishing absolute minimal requirements for various types of libraries, and sometimes in convincing the appropriate authorities that the library is underfunded, but are too general and imprecise to be used in the detailed evaluation of library services.

The Public Library Association did depart from the normal approach to deriving standards by developing and testing a "planning process" for public libraries (Palmour et al., 1980; McClure et al., 1987). While this planning process does contain evaluative elements, it is more concerned with the establishment of goals and objectives than it is with true evaluation of existing services.

Library Surveys

This is another topic touched upon in the author's earlier book but omitted here. The conduct of a library survey will typically involve the use of questionnaires or interviews applied to a sample of library users. Some pros and cons of various approaches are discussed in Martyn and Lancaster (1981). The librarian proposing such a study would be well advised to consult with a specialist on the design of survey instruments. The old standard on the wording of questionnaires is a book by Payne (1951). Many more recent books may also be found useful (see, for example, Berdie, 1986). A good summary of library "use studies," now somewhat out of date, was prepared by Tobin (1974).

Some data gathering techniques described by DeProspo et al. (1973) can be considered to be useful components of a library survey. One example of their application is described by Schrader (1980-1981)

Program Evaluation

A library may offer various programs that are beyond the scope of "traditional" services. Since such programs are of great diversity, each one presents a different problem in evaluation. Certain library programs, for example, might be evaluated through the use of techniques drawn from the field of education. Examples of the evaluation of specialized programs can be found in the work of Johnson (1986) on library literacy projects and of Chelton (1987) on the evaluation of programs (e.g., storytelling) for children.

Evaluation Data from Computer Systems

The application of computers to library operations allows the librarian to collect, on a continuous basis and at little cost, evaluation data that were difficult, if not impossible, to gather earlier. Some examples were discussed in the chapters on collection evaluation. Others can be found in Burns (1975), Overton (1979), Brophy (1986), and Lancaster (1983).

Some Final Evaluation Criteria

Writing in *The Chronicle of Higher Education*, two faculty members from Towson State University (Lev and Vatz, 1983) propose their own scale for the evaluation of academic libraries. Their evaluation criteria are:

—Percentage of volumes not missing
—Percentage of serials unmutilated
—Average decibels of noise per floor
—Number and percentage of working photocopy machines
—Incidence of eyestrain among microforms users
—Friendliness and helpfulness of library staff

As with Line's version of Ranganathan's Five Laws of Library Science, presented in Chapter 1, these criteria may seem merely facetious. They should not be dismissed too lightly. That users of libraries propose such criteria, even in jest, should prod librarians into the critical examination of their services and encourage them to perform objective studies designed to make their institution a growing organism rather than a growing mausoleum.

Study Questions

1. You are the newly appointed Director of Libraries for Black University. You have apparently inherited a rather difficult situation. The public service librarians report gross inefficiencies in the technical services area. They claim that procedures used for ordering, claiming, cataloging, and physical processing of books are duplicative, unnecessarily costly, and causing great delays in making materials accessible for use by patrons. You order a complete analysis of the technical processing department. How should the analysis be done?

2. A large university library has plans to introduce an integrated data processing system which will be a circulation system, on-line catalog, in-process file, and so on. The director of the library believes that this will be an excellent opportunity to build into the system a comprehensive evaluation component. She wants more than just analytical breakdowns of circulation. She wonders, in fact, if it might be possible to build in some form of continuous collection evaluation, catalog use study, and document delivery test. You have been asked to analyze the situation and advise her on how such evaluation components might be incorporated in the proposed system.

References

Aguilar, W. The application of relative use and interlibrary demand in collection development. *Collection Management*, 8, 1, 1986, 15-24.

Aguilar, W. *Relationship Between Classes of Books Circulated and Classes of Books Requested on Interlibrary Loan*. Doctoral thesis. Urbana, University of Illinois, Graduate School of Library and Information Science, 1984.

Allen, T.J. and Gerstberger, P.G. *Criteria for Selection of an Information Source*. Cambridge, Mass., Massachusetts Institute of Technology, Sloan School of Management, 1966. Another version appears in *Journal of Applied Psychology*, 52, 1968, 272-279.

Altman, E. et al. *A Data Gathering and Instructional Manual for Performance Measures in Public Libraries*. Chicago, Celadon Press, 1976.

American Library Association. *Catalog Use Study*, ed. by V. Mostecky. Chicago, American Library Association, 1958.

Baker, S.L. *An Exploration into Factors Causing the Increased Circulation of Displayed Books*. Doctoral thesis. Urbana, University of Illinois, Graduate School of Library and Information Science, 1985.

Ballard, T. Library systems: a concept that has failed us. *Wilson Library Bulletin*, 60, 4, 1985, 19-22.

Ballard, T. *The Failure of Resource Sharing in Public Libraries and Alternative Strategies for Service*. Chicago, American Library Association, 1986.

Baughman, J.C. A structural analysis of the literature of sociology. *Library Quarterly*, 44, 1974, 293-308.

Baumol, W.J. and Marcus, M. *Economics of Academic Libraries*. Washington, D.C., American Council of Education, 1973.

Benham, F. and Powell, R.R. *Success in Answering Reference Questions: Two Studies*. Metuchen, N.J., Scarecrow Press, 1987.

Bennion, B.C. and Karschamroon, S. Multivariate regression models for estimating journal usefulness in physics. *Journal of Documentation*, 40, 1984, 217-227.

Berdie, D.R. et al. *Questionnaires: design and use*. Metuchen, N.J., Scarecrow Press, 1986.

Betts, D.A. and Hargrave, R. *How Many Books?* Bradford, England, MCB Publications, 1982.

Birbeck, V.P. Unobtrusive testing of public library reference service. *Refer*, 4,2, 1986, 5-9.

Bland, R.N. The college textbook as a tool for collection evaluation, analysis, and retrospective collection development. *Library Acquisitions: Practice and Theory*, 4, 1980, 193-197.

Blau, P.M. and Margulies, R.Z. The reputation of American professional schools. *Change*, 6, 10, 1974-1975, 42-47.

Bommer, M.R.W. *The Development of a Management System for Effective Decision Making and Planning in a University Library.* Philadelphia, University of Pennsylvania, Wharton School of Finance and Commerce, 1973. (ERIC Document Reproduction Service No. ED 071 727).

Bommer, M.R.W. Review of *Performance Measures for Public Libraries. Library Quarterly*, 44, 1974, 273-275.

Bonn, G.S. Evaluation of the collection. *Library Trends*, 22, 1973-1974, 265-304.

Borkowski, C. and Macleod, M.J. The implications of some recent studies of library use. *Scholarly Publishing*, 11, 1979, 3-24.

Bourne, C.P. *Overlapping Coverage of Bibliography of Agriculture by 15 Other Secondary Sources.* Palo Alto, Information General Corporation, 1969.

Bourne, C.P. Some user requirements stated quantitatively in terms of the 90% library. In: *Electronic Information Handling*, ed. by A. Kent et al., pp. 93-110. Washington, D.C., Spartan Books, 1965.

Bourne, C.P. and Robinson, J. *SDI Citation Checking as a Measure of the Performance of Library Document Delivery Systems.* Berkeley, University of California at Berkeley, Institute of Library Research, 1973. (ERIC Document Reproduction Service No. ED 082 774).

Bradford, S.C. *Documentation.* London, Crosby Lockwood, 1948.

Braunstein, Y.M. Costs and benefits of library information: the user point of view. *Library Trends*, 28, Summer 1979, 79-87.

Broadus, R.N. The applications of citation analyses to library collection building. *Advances in Librarianship*, 7, 1977, 299-335.

Brookes, B.C. Obsolescence of special library periodicals: sampling errors and utility contours. *Journal of the American Society for Information Science*, 21, 1970, 320-329.

Brophy, P. *Management Information and Decision Support Systems in Libraries.* Aldershot, England, Gower Publishing Co., 1986.

Broude, J. Journal deselection in an academic environment: a comparison of faculty and librarian choices. *Serials Librarian*, 3, 1978, 147-166.

Buckland, M.K. *Book Availability and the Library User.* New York, Pergamon Press, 1975.

Buckland, M.K. An operations research study of a variable loan and duplication policy at the University of Lancaster. *Library Quarterly,* 42, 1972, 97-106.

Buckland, M.K. and Hindle, A. Loan policies, duplication and availability. In: *Planning Library Services;* ed. by A.G. Mackenzie and I.M. Stuart, pp. 1-16. Lancaster, University of Lancaster Library, 1969.

Buckland, M.K. et al. Methodological problems in assessing the overlap between bibliographic files and library holdings. *Information Processing and Management,* 11, 1975, 89-105.

Buckland, M.K. et al. *Systems Analysis of a University Library.* Lancaster, University of Lancaster Library, 1970.

Bunge, C.A. *Professional Education and Reference Efficiency.* Springfield, Illinois State Library, 1967.

Burns, R.W., Jr. *Library Performance Measures as Seen in the Descriptive Statistics Generated by a Computer Managed Circulation System.* 1975. (ERIC Document Reproduction Service No. ED 115 252).

Burr, R.L. Evaluating library collections: a case study. *Journal of Academic Librarianship,* 5, 1979, 256-260.

Burton, R.E. and Kebler, R.W. The "half-life" of some scientific and technical literatures. *American Documentation,* 11, 1960, 18-22.

Buzzard, M.L. and New, D.E. An investigation of collection support for doctoral research. *College and Research Libraries,* 44, 1983, 469-475.

Byrd, G.D. et al. Collection development using interlibrary loan borrowing and acquisitions statistics. *Bulletin of the Medical Library Association,* 70, 1982, 1-9.

Carlson, G.*Search Strategy by Reference Librarians. Part 3 of Final Report on the Organization of Large Files.* Sherman Oaks, Calif., Hughes Dynamics Inc., Advanced Information Systems Division, 1964. PB 166192.

Chelton, M.K. Evaluation of children's services. *Library Trends,* 35, 1987, 463-484.

Chen, C.C. The use patterns of physics journals in a large academic research library. *Journal of the American Society for Information Science,* 23, 1972, 254-270.

Childers, T. *The Effectiveness of Information Service in Public Libraries: Suffolk County.* Philadelphia, Drexel University, School of Library and Information Science, 1978. A condensed version appears in *Library Journal,* April 15, 1980, 924-928.

Childers, T. Managing the quality of reference/information service. *Library Quarterly,* 42, 1972, 212-217.

Ciliberti, A.C. et al. Material availability: a study of academic library performance. *College and Research Libraries,* 48, 1987, 513-527.

Citron, H.R. and Dodd, J.B. Cost allocation and cost recovery considerations in a special academic library: Georgia Institute of Technology. *Science and Technology Libraries,* 5, 2, 1984, 1-14.

Clapp, V.W. and Jordan, R.T. Quantitative criteria for adequacy of academic library collections. *College and Research Libraries,* 26, 1965, 371-380.

Clark, P.M. *A Study to Refine and Test New Measures of Library Service and Train Library Personnel in Their Use.* New Brunswick, N.J., Rutgers, the State University, Bureau of Library and Information Science Research, 1976. (ERIC Document Reproduction Service No. ED 138 262).

Coale, R.P. Evaluation of a research library collection: Latin-American colonial history at the Newberry. *Library Quarterly,* 35, 1965, 173-184.

Comer, C. List-checking as a method for evaluating library collections. *Collection Building,* 3, 3, 1981, 26-34.

Cooper, M. Current information dissemination: ideas and practices. *Journal of Chemical Documentation,* 8, 1968, 207-218.

Cooper, W.S. Expected search length: a single measure of retrieval effectiveness based on the weak ordering action of retrieval systems. *American Documentation,* 19, 1968, 30-41.

Council of Federal Libraries. *Performance Measurement in Federal Libraries: A Handbook.* Ottawa, National Library of Canada, 1979.

Cronin, M.T. *Performance Measurement for Public Services in Academic and Research Libraries.* Washington, D.C., Association of Research Libraries, 1985.

Crowley, T. Half-right reference: is it true? *RQ,* 25, 1985, 59-68.

Crowley, T. Referred reference questions: how well are they answered? In: *Evaluation of Reference Services;* ed. by W. Katz and R.A. Fraley, pp. 83-93. New York, Haworth Press, 1984.

Crowley, T. and Childers, T. *Information Service in Public Libraries: Two Studies.* Metuchen, N.J., Scarecrow Press, 1971.

Daiute, R.J. and Gorman, K.A. *Library Operations Research.* Dobbs Ferry, N.Y., Oceana Publications, 1974.

De Prospo, E.R. et al. *Performance Measures for Public Libraries.* Chicago, Public Library Association, 1973.

Detweiler, M.J. Availability of materials in public libraries. In: *Library Effectiveness: a State of the Art,* pp. 75-83. Chicago, American Library Association, 1980.

Detweiler, M.J. The "best size" public library. *Library Journal,* 111, May 15, 1986, 34-35.

Dickson, J. An analysis of user errors in searching an online catalog. *Cataloging & Classification Quarterly,* 4, 3, 1984, 19-38.

Divilbiss, J.L. and Self, P.C. Work analysis by random sampling. *Bulletin of the Medical Library Association,* 66, 1978, 19-23.

Doll, C.A. *A Study of Overlap and Duplication Among Children's Collections in Public and Elementary School Libraries.* Doctoral thesis. Urbana, University of Illinois, Graduate School of Library and Information Science, 1980.

Domas, R.E. *Correlating the Classes of Books Taken Out Of and Books Used Within an Open-Stack Library.* San Antonio, San Antonio College Library, 1978. (ERIC Document Reproduction Service No. ED 171 282).

Dowlin, K. and Magrath, L. Beyond the numbers—a decision support system. In: *Library Automation as a Source of Management Information;* ed. by F.W. Lancaster, pp. 27-58. Urbana, University of Illinois, Graduate School of Library and Information Science, 1983.

Drone, J.M. *A Study of the Relationship Between Size of Monographic Collections and Internal Duplication in a Select Group of Libraries Using LCS (Library Computer System).* Doctoral thesis. Urbana, University of Illinois, Graduate School of Library and Information Science, 1984.

Drucker, P.F. Managing the public service institution. *The Public Interest,* 33, Fall, 1973, 43-60.

Elchesen, D.R. Cost-effectiveness comparison of manual and on-line retrospective bibliographic searching. *Journal of the American Society for Information Science,* 29, 1978, 56-66.

Ellsworth, R. *The Economics of Compact Storage.* Metuchen, N.J., Scarecrow Press, 1969.

Estabrook, L.S. Valuing a document delivery system. *RQ,* 26, 1986, 58-62.

Ettelt, H.J. Book use at a small (very) community college library. *Library Journal,* 103, 1978, 2314-2315.

Evans, G.T. and Beilby, A. A library management information system in a multi-campus environment. In: *Library Automation as a Source of Management Information;* ed. by F.W. Lancaster, pp. 164-196. Urbana, University of Illinois, Graduate School of Library and Information Science, 1983.

Fairthorne, R.A. Empirical hyperbolic distributions (Bradford-Zipf-Mandelbrot) for bibliometric description and prediction. *Journal of Documentation,* 25, 1969, 319-343.

Ferguson, D. et al. The CLR public online catalog study: an overview. *Information Technology and Libraries,* 1, 1982, 84-97.

Flynn, R.R. The University of Pittsburgh study of journal usage: a summary report. *Serials Librarian,* 4, 1979, 25-33.

Freeman & Co. *Final Report on a Library Systems Study.* Palo Alto, Freeman & Co., 1965.

Frohmberg, K.A. et al. Increases in book availability in a large college library. *Proceedings of the American Society for Information Science,* 17, 1980, 292-294.

Fussler, H.H. and Simon, J.L. *Patterns in the Use of Books in Large Research Libraries.* Chicago, University of Chicago Press, 1969.

Gabriel, M.R. Online collection evaluation, course by course. *Collection Building,* 8, 2, 1987, 20-24.

Garfield, E. Which medical journals have the greatest impact? *Annals of Internal Medicine,* 105, 1986, 313-320.

Gers, R. and Seward, L.J. Improving reference performance: results of a statewide study. *Library Journal,* 110, 18, 1985, 32-35.

Getz, M. *Public Libraries: an Economic View.* Baltimore, Johns Hopkins University Press, 1980.

Gillentine, J. et al. *Evaluating Library Services.* Santa Fe, New Mexico State Library, 1981.

Goehlert, R. Book availability and delivery service. *Journal of Academic Librarianship,* 4, 1978, 368-371.

Goehlert, R. The effect of loan policies on circulation recalls. *Journal of Academic Librarianship,* 5, 1979, 79-82.

Golden, B. A method for quantitatively evaluating a university library collection. *Library Resources and Technical Services,* 18, 1974, 268-274.

Goldhor, H. Analysis of an inductive method of evaluating the book colection of a public library. *Libri,* 23, 1973, 6-17.

Goldhor, H. The effect of prime display location on public library circulation of selected adult titles. *Library Quarterly,* 42, 1972, 371-389.

Goldhor, H. Experimental effects on the choice of books borrowed by public library adult patrons. *Library Quarterly,* 51, 1981a, 253-268.

Goldhor, H. *A Plan for the Development of Public Library Service in the Minneapolis-Saint Paul Metropolitan Area.* Minneapolis, Metropolitan Library Service Agency, 1967.

Goldhor, H. A report on an application of the inductive method of evaluation of public library books. *Libri,* 31, 1981b, 121-129.

Gore, D. Let them eat cake while reading catalog cards: an essay on the availability problem. *Library Journal,* 100, 1975, 93-98.

Gouke, M.N. and Pease, S. Title searches in an online catalog and a card catalog. *Journal of Academic Librarianship,* 8, 1982, 137-143.

Griscom, R. Periodical use in a university music library: a citation study of theses and dissertations submitted to the Indiana University School of Music from 1975-1980. *Serials Librarian,* 7, 3, 1983, 35-52.

Groos, O.V. Citation characteristics of astronomical literature. *Journal of Documentation*, 25, 1969, 344-347.

Hafner, A.W. Primary journal selection using citations from an indexing service journal: a method and example from nursing literature. *Bulletin of the Medical Library Association*, 64, 1976, 392-401.

Hall, B.H. *Collection Assessment Manual for College and University Libraries*. Phoenix, Oryx Press, 1985.

Hamburg, M. et al. *Library Planning and Decision-Making Systems*. Cambridge, Mass., MIT Press, 1974.

Hardesty, L. Use of library materials at a small liberal arts college. *Library Research*, 3, 1981, 261-282.

Harris, C. A comparison of issues and in-library use of books. *ASLIB Proceedings*, 29, 1977, 118-126.

Harris, I.W. *The Influence of Accessibility on Academic Library Use*. Doctoral thesis. New Brunswick, Rutgers, The State University, 1966.

Hawkins, D.T. The percentage distribution: a method of ranking journals. *Proceedings of the American Society for Information Science*, 16, 1979, 230-235.

Hayes, R.M. The distribution of use of library materials: analysis of data from the University of Pittsburgh. *Library Research*, 3, 1981, 215-260.

Hernon, P. and McClure, C.R. Quality of data issues in unobtrusive testing of library reference service: recommendations and strategies. *Library and Information Science Research*, 9, 1987, 77-93.

Hindle, A. and Buckland, M.K. In-library book usage in relation to circulation. *Collection Management*, 2, 1978, 265-277.

Holland, M.P. Serial cuts vs. public service: a formula. *College and Research Libraries*, 37, 1976, 543-548.

Jain, A.K. *Report on a Statistical Study of Book Use*. Lafayette, Ind., Purdue University, School of Industrial Engineering, 1967.

Jain, A.K. *A Sampled Data Study of Book Usage in the Purdue University Libraries*. Lafayette, Ind., Purdue University, 1965.

Jain, A.K. Sampling and data collection methods for a book-use study. *Library Quarterly*, 39, 1969, 245-252.

Jain, A.K. Sampling and short-period usage in the Purdue Library. *College and Research Libraries*, 27, 1966, 211-218.

Jenks, G.M. Circulation and its relationship to the book collection and academic departments. *College and Research Libraries*, 37, 1976, 145-152.

Jensen, R.J. et al. Costs and benefits to industry of online literature searches. *Special Libraries*, 71, 1980, 291-299.

Johnson, C.A. and Trueswell, R.W. The weighted criteria statistic score: an approach to journal selection. *College and Research Libraries*, 39, 1978, 287-292.

Johnson, D.W. Evaluation of library literacy projects. *Library Trends*, 35, 1986, 311-326.

Jones, R.M. Improving OKAPI: transaction log analysis of failed searches in an online catalogue. *Vine*, 62, 1986, 3-13.

Jordan, R.T. Library characteristics of colleges ranking high in academic excellence. *College and Research Libraries*, 24, 1963, 369-376.

Kantor, P.B. Availability analysis. *Journal of the American Society for Information Science*, 27, 1976, 311-319.

Kantor, P.B. Demand-adjusted shelf availability parameters. *Journal of Academic Librarianship*, 7, 1981, 78-82.

Kantor, P.B. The library as an information utility in the university context: evolution and measurement of service. *Journal of the American Society for Information Science*, 27, 1976, 100-112.

Kantor, P.B. Vitality: an indirect measure of relevance. *Collection Management*, 2, 1978, 83-95.

Kaske,N.K. and Sanders, N.P. *Study of Online Public Access Catalogs: an Overview and Application of Findings.* Dublin, Ohio, Online Computer Library Center, 1983.

Kennedy, R.A. Computer-derived management information in a special library. In: *Library Automation as a Source of Management Information;* ed. by F.W. Lancaster, pp. 128-147. Urbana, University of Illinois, Graduate School of Library and Information Science, 1983.

Kent, A. et al. *Use of Library Materials: the University of Pittsburgh Study.* New York, Dekker, 1979.

King, D.W. Pricing policies in academic libraries. *Library Trends*, 28, Summer 1979, 47-62.

King, D.W. et al. *Statistical Indicators of Scientific and Technical Communication.* Vol. 2. Rockville, Md., King Research, Inc., 1976.

King, G.B. and Berry, R. *Evaluation of the University of Minnesota Libraries Reference Department Telephone Information Service. Pilot Study.* Minneapolis, University of Minnesota, Library School, 1973. (ERIC Document Reproduction Service No. ED 077 517).

King Research Inc. *Value of the Energy Data Base.* Rockville, Md., 1982.

Kramer, J. How to survive in industry: cost justifying library services. *Special Libraries*, 62, 1971, 487-489.

Krueger, K. *Coordinated Cooperative Collection Development for Illinois Libraries.* Springfield, Illinois State Library, 1983. 3 vols.

Lancaster, F.W. Evaluating collections by their use. *Collection Management*, 4, 1/2, 1982, 15-43.

Lancaster, F.W. *Information Retrieval Systems: Characteristics, Testing and Evaluation.* Second edition. New York, Wiley, 1979.

Lancaster, F.W. *The Measurement and Evaluation of Library Services.* Washington, D.C., Information Resources Press, 1977.

Lancaster, F.W. Some considerations relating to the cost-effectiveness of online services in libraries. *Aslib Proceedings,* 33, 1981, 10-14.

Lancaster, F.W., ed. *Library Automation as a Source of Management Information.* Urbana, University of Illinois, Graduate School of Library and Information Science, 1983. (Proceedings of the Nineteenth Annual Clinic on Library Applications of Data Processing).

Lancaster, F.W. and Mehrotra, R. The five laws of library science as a guide to the evaluation of library services. In: *Perspectives in Library and Information Science.* Vol. 1, pp. 26-39. Lucknow, Print House, 1982.

Lawrence, G.S. and Oja, A.R. *The Use of General Collections at the University of California.* Sacramento, California State Department of Education, 1980. (ERIC Document Reproduction Service No. ED 191 490).

Leimkuhler, F.F. Systems analysis in university libraries. *College and Research Libraries,* 27, 1966, 13-18.

Lev, P. and Vatz, R. How to measure quality of life in libraries. *The Chronicle of Higher Education,* April 6, 1983, page 33.

Lewis, D.W. Research on the use of online catalogs and its implications for library practice. *Journal of Academic Librarianship,* 13, 1987, 152-157.

Line, M.B. The ability of a university library to provide books wanted by researchers. *Journal of Librarianship,* 5, 1973, 37-51.

Line, M.B. Citation analyses: a note. *International Library Review,* 9, 1977, 429.

Line, M.B. Rank lists based on citations and library uses as indicators of journal usage in individual libraries. *Collection Management,* 2, 1978, 313-316.

Line, M.B. Review of *Use of Library Materials: the University of Pittsburgh Study.* College and Research Libraries, 40, 1979, 557-558.

Line, M.B. and Sandison, A. "Obsolescence" and changes in the use of literature with time. *Journal of Documentation,* 30, 1974, 283-350.

Lipetz, B.A. Catalog use in a large research library. *Library Quarterly,* 42, 1972, 129-139.

Lipetz, B.A. *User Requirements in Identifying Desired Works in a Large Library.* New Haven, Yale University Library, 1970.

Lipetz, B.A. and Paulson, P.J. A study of the impact of introducing an online subject catalog at the New York State Library. *Library Trends,* 35, 1987, 597-617.

Lister, W.C. *Least Cost Decision Rules for the Selection of Library Materials for Compact Storage.* Doctoral thesis. Lafayette, Ind., Purdue University, School of Industrial Engineering, 1967. PB 174 441.

Longo, R.M.J. and Machado, U.D. Characterization of databases in agricultural sciences. *Journal of the American Society for Information Science*, 32, 1981, 83-91.

Longyear, R.M. Article citation and "obsolescence" in musicological journals. *Notes*, 33, 1977, 563-571.

Lopez, M.D. The Lopez or citation technique of in-depth collection evaluation explicated. *College and Research Libraries*, 44, 3, 1983, 251-255.

Magson, M.S. Techniques for the measurement of cost-benefit in information centres. *Aslib Proceedings*, 25, 1973, 164-185.

Maltby, A. Measuring catalogue utility. *Journal of Librarianship*, 3, 1971, 180-189.

Maltby, A. *U.K. Catalogue Use Survey: a Report.* London, Library Association, 1973.

Mankin, C.J. and Bastille, J.D. An analysis of the differences between density-of-use ranking and raw-use ranking of library journal use. *Journal of the American Society for Information Science*, 32, 1981, 224-228.

Mansbridge, J. Availability studies in libraries. *Library and Information Science Research*, 8, 1986, 299-314.

Mansbridge, J. *Evaluating Resource Sharing Library Networks.* Doctoral thesis. Cleveland, Case Western Reserve University, 1984.

Markey, K. *The Process of Subject Searching in the Library Catalog: Final Report of the Subject Access Research Project.* Dublin, Ohio, Online Computer Library Center, 1983.

Markey, K. *Subject Searching in Library Catalogs.* Dublin, Ohio, Online Computer Library Center, 1984.

Martyn, J. Tests on abstracts journals: coverage, overlap, and indexing. *Journal of Documentation*, 23, 1967, 45-70.

Martyn, J. Unintentional duplication of research. *New Scientist*, 21, 1964, 338.

Martyn, J. and Lancaster, F.W. *Investigative Methods in Library and Information Science: an Introduction.* Washington, D.C., Information Resources Press, 1981.

Martyn, J. and Slater, M. Tests on abstracts journals. *Journal of Documentation*, 20, 1964, 212-235.

Mason, D. PPBS: application to an industrial information and library service. *Journal of Librarianship*, 4, 1972, 91-105.

McCain, K.W. and Bobick, J.E. Patterns of journal use in a departmental library: a citation analysis. *Journal of the American Society for Information Science*, 32, 1981, 257-267.

McClellan, A.W. *The Logistics of Public Library Bookstock.* London, Association of Assistant Librarians, 1978.

McClellan, A.W. New concepts of service. *Library Association Record,* 1956, 299-305.

McClure, C.R. and Hernon, P. *Improving the Quality of Reference Service for Government Publications.* Chicago, American Library Association, 1983.

McClure, C.R. et al. *Planning & Role Setting for Public Libraries: a Manual of Options and Procedures.* Chicago, American Library Association, 1987.

McDonough, A.M. *Information Economics and Management Systems.* McGraw-Hill, New York, 1963.

McGrath, W.E. Correlating the subjects of books taken out of and books used within an open-stack library. *College and Research Libraries,* 32, 1971, 280-285.

McGrath, W.E. Measuring classified circulation according to curriculum. *College and Research Libraries,* 29, 1968, 347-350.

McGrath, W.E. The significance of books used according to a classified profile of academic departments. *College and Research Libraries,* 33, 1972, 212-219.

McGrath, W.E. et al. Ethnocentricity and cross-disciplinary circulation. *College and Research Libraries,* 40, 1979, 511-518.

McInnis, R.M. The formula approach to library size: an empirical study of its efficacy in evaluating research libraries. *College and Research Libraries,* 33, 1972, 190-198.

Metz, P. Duplication in library collections: what we know and what we need to know. *Collection Building,* 2, 3, 1980, 27-33.

Metz, P. *The Landscape of Literatures: Use of Subject Collections in a Library.* Chicago, American Library Association, 1983.

Mills, T.R. *The University of Illinois Film Center collection use study.* 1982. (ERIC Document Reproduction Service No. ED 227 821).

Molyneux, R.E. Patterns, processes of growth, and the projection of library size: a critical review of the literature on academic library growth. *Library and Information Science Research,* 8, 1986, 5-28.

Mooers, C.N. Mooers' Law or, why some retrieval systems are used and others are not. *American Documentation,* 11, 3, 1960, ii.

Morse, P.M. Demand for library materials: an exercise in probability analysis. *Collection Management,* 1, 1976-1977, 47-78.

Mosher, P.H. Quality and library collections: new directions in research and practice in collection evaluation. *Advances in Librarianship,* 13, 1984, 211-238.

Mostyn, G.R. The use of supply-demand equality in evaluating collection adequacy. *California Librarian,* 35, 1974, 16-23.

Mount, E. ed. *Weeding of Collections in Sci-Tech Libraries.* New York, Haworth Press, 1986. (Also published as *Science and Technology Libraries,* 6, Number 3, Spring 1986.)

Mueller, E. Are new books read more than old ones? *Library Quarterly,* 35, 1965, 166-172.

Mueller, M.W. *Time, Cost and Value Factors in Information Retrieval.* Paper presented at the IBM Information Systems Conference, Poughkeepsie, N.Y., September 21-23, 1959.

Murfin, M.E. The myth of accessibility: frustration and failure in retrieving periodicals. *Journal of Academic Librarianship,* 6, 1980, 16-19.

Myers, M.J. and Jirjees, J.M. *The Accuracy of Telephone Reference/Information Services in Academic Libraries.* Metuchen, N.J., Scarecrow Press, 1983.

Narin, F. *Evaluative Bibliometrics.* Cherry Hill, N.J., Computer Horizons, Inc., 1976. PB 252 339.

Newhouse, J.P. and Alexander, A.J. *An Economic Analysis of Public Library Services.* Lexington, Mass., Lexington Books, 1972.

Nightingale, R.A. A cost-benefit study of a manually-produced current awareness bulletin. *ASLIB Proceedings,* 25, 1973, 153-157.

Nimmer, R.J. Circulation and collection patterns at the Ohio State University Libraries 1973-1977. *Library Acquisitions: Practice and Theory,* 4, 1980, 61-70.

Nisonger, T.E. An in-depth collection evaluation at the University of Manitoba Library: a test of the Lopez method. *Library Resources and Technical Services,* 24, 1980, 329-338.

Nisonger, T.E. A test of two citation checking techniques for evaluating political science collections in university libraries. *Library Resources and Technical Services,* 27, 1983, 163-176.

O'Connor, D.O. Evaluating public libraries using standard scores: the library quotient. *Library Research,* 4, 1982, 51-70.

Olson, E.E. *Survey of User Service Policies in Indiana Libraries and Information Centers.* Bloomington, Indiana State Library, 1970.

Olson, L.M. Reference service evaluation in medium-sized academic libraries: a model. *Journal of Academic Librarianship,* 9, 1984, 322-329.

Orr, R.H. and Olson, E.E. *Quantitative Measures as Management Tools.* Materials prepared for use in a continuing education course, CE 7, of the Medical Library Association. Chicago, Medical Library Association, 1968.

Orr, R.H. and Schless, A.P. Document delivery capabilities of major biomedical libraries in 1968: results of a national survey employing standardized tests. *Bulletin of the Medical Library Association,* 60, 1972, 382-422.

Orr, R.H. et al. Development of methodologic tools for planning and managing library services. II. Measuring a library's capability for providing documents. *Bulletin of the Medical Library Association,* 56, 1968a, 241-267.

Orr, R.H. et al. Development of methodologic tools for planning and managing library services. III. Standardized inventories of library services. *Bulletin of the Medical Library Association,* 56, 1968b, 380-403.

Overton, C.M. *Review of Management Information from Computer-Based Circulation Systems in Academic Libraries.* London, The British Library, 1979.

Palmour, V.E. et al. *A Planning Process for Public Libraries.* Chicago, American Library Association, 1980.

Pan, E. Journal citation as a predictor of journal usage in libraries. *Collection Management,* 2, 1978, 29-38.

Payne, S.L. *The Art of Asking Questions.* Princeton, N.J., Princeton University Press, 1951.

Peat, W.L. The use of research libraries: a comment about the Pittsburgh study and its critics. *Journal of Academic Librarianship,* 7, 1981, 229-231.

Peat, Marwick, Mitchell & Co. *California Public Library Systems: a Comprehensive Review with Guidelines for the Next Decade.* Los Angeles, 1975.

Penner, R.J. Measuring a library's capability. *Journal of Education for Librarianship,* 13, 1972, 17-30.

Perk, L.J. and Van Pulis, N. Periodical usage in an education-psychology library. *College and Research Libraries,* 38, 1977, 304-308.

Pings, V. A study of the use of materials circulated from an engineering library. *American Documentation,* 18, 1967, 178-184.

Piternick, G. Library growth and academic quality. *College and Research Libraries,* 24, 1963, 223-229.

Pizer, I.H. and Cain, A.M. Objective tests of library performance. *Special Libraries,* 59, 1968, 704-711.

Plate, K.H. *Cost Justification of Information Services.* Studio City, California, Cibbarelli and Associates Inc., 1983.

Popovich, C.J. The characteristics of a collection for research in business/management. *College and Research Libraries,* 39, 1978, 110-117.

Porta, M.A. and Lancaster, F.W. Evaluation of a scholarly collection in a specific subject area by bibliographic checking. *Libri,* 38, 1988 (in press).

Potter, W.G. Studies of collection overlap: a literature review. *Library Research,* 4, 1982, 3-21.

Powell, R.R. *An Investigation of the Relationship Between Reference Collection Size and Other Reference Service Factors and Success in Answering Reference Questions.* Doctoral thesis. University of Illinois, Graduate School of Library Science, 1976. A condensed version appears in *Library Quarterly,* 48, 1978, 1-19. [For another version see Benham and Powell (1987)].

Powell, R.R. Reference effectiveness: a review of research. *Library and Information Science Research,* 6, 1984, 3-19.

Power, C.J. and Bell, G.H. Automated circulation, patron satisfaction, and collection evaluation in academic libraries—a circulation analysis formula. *Journal of Library Automation,* 11, 1978, 366-369.

Price, D.J. The citation cycle. In: *Key Papers in Information Science;* ed. by B.C. Griffith, pp. 195-210. White Plains, N.Y., Knowledge Industry Publications, 1980.

Raffel, J.A. and Shishko, R. *Systematic Analysis of University Libraries.* Cambridge, Mass., MIT Press, 1969.

Ramsden, M.J. *Performance Measurement of Some Melbourne Public Libraries.* Melbourne, Library Council of Victoria, 1978.

Ranganathan, S.R. *The Five Laws of Library Science.* Bombay, Asia Publishing House, 1931.

Rice, B.A. Selection and evaluation of chemistry periodicals. *Science and Technology Libraries,* 4, 1, 1983, 43-59.

Roberts, S.A., ed. *Costing and the Economics of Library and Information Services.* London, Aslib, 1984.

Robertson, S.E. The parametric description of retrieval tests. *Journal of Documentation,* 25, 1969, 93-107.

Rodger, E.J. and Goodwin, J. *Reference Accuracy at the Fairfax County Public Library.* Washington, D.C., Metropolitan Washington Library Council, 1984.

Rogers, E.M. and Shoemaker, F.F. *Communication of Innovations.* Second edition. New York, Free Press, 1971.

Rosenberg, K.C. Evaluation of an industrial library: a simple-minded technique. *Special Libraries,* 60, 1969, 635-638.

Rosenberg, P. *Cost Finding for Public Libraries.* Chicago, American Library Association, 1985.

Rosenberg, V. *The Application of Psychometric Techniques to Determine the Attitudes of Individuals Toward Information Seeking.* Bethlehem, Pa., Lehigh University, Center for Information Sciences, 1966. Another version appears in *Information Storage and Retrieval,* 3, 1967, 119-127.

Rubin, R. *Inhouse Use of Materials in Public Libraries.* Urbana, University of Illinois, Graduate School of Library and Information Science, 1986.

Sandison, A. Densities of use, and absence of obsolescence, in physics journals at MIT. *Journal of the American Society for Information Science,* 25, 1974, 172-182.

Sandison, A. Obsolescence in biomedical journals. *Library Research,* 2, 1981, 347-348.

Saracevic, T. et al. Causes and dynamics of user frustration in an academic library. *College and Research Libraries,* 38, 1977, 7-18.

Sargent, S.H. The uses and limitations of Trueswell. *College and Research Libraries,* 40, 1979, 416-423.

Satariano, W.A. Journal use in sociology: citation analysis versus readership patterns. *Library Quarterly,* 48, 1978, 293-300.

Scales, P.A. Citation analyses as indicators of the use of serials: a comparison of ranked title lists produced by citation counting and from use data. *Journal of Documentation,* 32, 1976, 17-25.

Schad, J.G. Missing the brass ring in the iron city. *Journal of Academic Librarianship,* 5, 1979, 60-63.

Schauer, B.P. *The Economics of Managing Library Service.* Chicago, American Library Association, 1986.

Schloman, B.F. and Ahl, R.E. Retention periods for journals in a small academic library. *Special Libraries,* 70, 1979, 377-383.

Schmidt, J. Evaluation of reference service in college libraries, in New South Wales, Australia. In: *Library Effectiveness: a State of the Art,* pp. 265-294. Chicago, American Library Association, 1980.

Schofield, J.L. et al. Evaluation of an academic library's stock effectiveness. *Journal of Librarianship,* 7, 1975, 207-227.

Schrader, A.M. Performance measures for public libraries: refinements in methodology and reporting. *Library Research,* 2, 1980-1981, 129-155.

Schwarz, P. Demand-adjusted shelf availability parameters: a second look. *College and Research Libraries,* 44, 4, 1983, 210-219.

Seba, D.B. and Forrest, B. Using SDI's to get primary journals: a new online way. *Online,* 2, 1, 1978, 10-15.

Shaw, W.M., Jr. A journal resource sharing strategy. *Library Research,* 1, 1979, 19-29.

Shaw, W.M., Jr. Longitudinal studies of book availability. In: *Library Effectiveness: a State of the Art,* pp. 338-349. Chicago, American Library Association, 1980.

Shaw, W.M. Jr. A practical journal usage technique. *College and Research Libraries,* 39, 1978, 479-484.

Simon, J.L. How many books should be stored where? an economic analysis. *College and Research Libraries,* 28, 1967, 93-103.

Slote, S.J. *Weeding Library Collections.* Second edition. Littleton, Colorado, Libraries Unlimited, 1982.

Smith, R.H. and Granade, W. User and library failures in an undergraduate library. *College and Research Libraries,* 39, 1978, 467-473.

Snowball, G.J. and Sampedro, J. Selection of periodicals for return to prime space from a storage facility. *Canadian Library Journal,* 30, 1973, 490-492.

Solomin, V.M. Efficiency indexes for the performance of information agencies. *Nauchno-Teknicheskaya Informatsiya,* series 1, number 5, 1974, 3-7. English translation appears in *Scientific and Technical Information Processing,* 1, 1974, 16-23.

Soper, M.E. *The Relationship Between Personal Collections and the Selection of Cited References.* Doctoral thesis. Urbana, University of Illinois, Graduate School of Library Science, 1972. A condensed version appears in *Library Quarterly,* 46, 1976, 397-415.

Sparck, Jones, K. *Information Retrieval Experiment.* London, Butterworths, 1981.

Spaulding, F.H. and Stanton, R.O. Computer-aided selection in a library network. *Journal of the American Society for Information Science,* 27, 1976, 269-280.

Specht, J. Patron use of an online circulation system in known-item searching. *Journal of the American Society for Information Science,* 31, 1980, 335-346.

Spencer, C.C. How to allocate personnel costs of reference. In: *Proceedings of the Symposium on Measurement of Reference;* ed. by K. Emerson, pp. 35-41. Chicago, American Library Association, 1974.

Spencer, C.C. Random time sampling with self-observation for library cost studies: unit costs of interlibrary loans and photocopies at a regional medical library. *Journal of the American Society for Information Science,* 22, 1971, 153-160.

Sprules, M.L. Online bibliometrics in an academic library. *Online,* 7, 1983, 25-34.

Standards for college libraries, 1986. *College and Research Libraries News,* 47, 1986, 189-200.

Stankus, T. and Rice, B. Handle with care: use and citation data for science journal management. *Collection Management,* 4, 1982, 95-110.

Stenstrom, P. and McBride, R.B. Serial use by social science faculty: a survey. *College and Research Libraries,* 40, 1979, 426-431.

Stinson, E.R. and Lancaster, F.W. Synchronous versus diachronous methods in the measurement of obsolescence by citation studies. *Journal of Information Science,* 13, 1987, 65-74.

Stoljarov, J.N. Optimum size of public library stocks. *Unesco Bulletin for Libraries,* 27, 1973, 22-28, 42.

Strain, P.M. A study of the usage and retention of technical periodicals. *Library Resources and Technical Services,* 10, 1966, 295-304.

Sullivan, M.V. et al. Obsolescence in biomedical journals: not an artifact of literature growth. *Library Research,* 2, 1980-1981, 29-45.

Swanson, D.R. Subjective versus objective relevance in bibliographic retrieval systems. *Library Quarterly,* 56, 1986, 389-398.

Tagliacozzo, R. and Kochen, M. Information-seeking behavior of catalog users. *Information Storage and Retrieval,* 6, 1970, 363-381.

Tagliacozzo, R. et al. Access and recognition: from users' data to catalogue entries. *Journal of Documentation,* 26, 1970, 230-249.

Taylor, C.R. A practical solution to weeding university library periodicals collections. *Collection Management,* 1, 1976-1977, 27-45.

Tobin, J.C. A study of library "use studies". *Information Storage and Retrieval,* 10, 1974, 101-113.

Torr, D.V. et al. *Program Studies on the Use of Published Indexes.* Bethesda, Md., General Electric Co., 1966. 2 vols.

Travillian, M. Peer coaching to improve reference performance in Maryland. *CLENEXCHANGE,* 11, 1985, 2-3.

Trochim, M.K. et al. *Measuring the Circulation Use of a Smalle Academic Library Collection: a Manual.* Chicago, Associated Colleges of the Midwest, 1980. [An updated version was issued by the Office of Management Studies, Association of Research Libraries in 1985.]

Trubkin, L. Building a core collection of business and management periodicals: how databases can help. *Online,* 6, 4, 1982, 43-49.

Trueswell, R.W. Determining the optimal number of volumes of a library's core collection. *Libri,* 16, 1966, 49-60.

Trueswell, R.W. A quantitative measure of user circulation requirements and its possible effect on stack thinning and multiple copy determination. *American Documentation,* 16, 1965, 20-25.

Trueswell, R.W. Two characteristics of circulation and their effect on the implementation of mechanized circulation control systems. *College and Research Libraries,* 25, 1964, 285-291.

Trueswell, R.W. User circulation satisfaction vs. size of holdings at three academic libraries. *College and Research Libraries,* 30, 1969, 204-213.

University of Chicago. Graduate Library School. *Requirements Study for Future Catalogs. Progress Report No. 2.* Chicago, 1968.

Urquhart, J.A. and Schofield, J.L. Measuring readers' failure at the shelf. *Journal of Documentation,* 27, 1971, 272-286.

Urquhart, J.A. and Schofield, J.L. Measuring readers' failure at the shelf in three university libraries. *Journal of Documentation,* 28, 1972, 233-241.

Urquhart, J.A. and Urquhart, N.C. *Relegation and Stock Control in Libraries.* Newcastle upon Tyne, Oriel Press, 1976.

Van House, N.A. *Output Measure for Public Libraries: a Manual of Standardized Procedures.* Second edition. Chicago, American Library Association, 1987.

Van Styvendaele, B.J.H. University scientists as seekers of information: sources of references to books and their first use versus date of publication. *Journal of Librarianship,* 13, 1981, 83-92.

Voigt, M.J. Acquisition rates in university libraries. *College and Research Libraries,* 36, 1975, 263-271.

Voigt, M.J. Circulation studies cannot reflect research use. *Journal of Academic Librarianship,* 5, 1979, 66.

Wainwright, E.J. and Dean, J.E. *Measure of Adequacy for Library Collections in Australian Colleges of Advanced Education.* Perth, Western Australian Institute of Technology, 1976. 2 vols.

Wallace, D.P. *An Index of Quality of Illinois Public Library Service.* Springfield, Illinois State Library, 1983.

Weech, T.L. and Goldhor, H. Obtrusive versus unobtrusive evaluation of reference service in five Illinois public libraries: a pilot study. *Library Quarterly,* 52, 1982, 305-324.

Wenger, C.B. and Childress, J. Journal evaluation in a large research library. *Journal of the American Society for Information Science,* 28, 1977, 293-299.

Wenger, C.B. et al. Monograph evaluation for acquisitions in a large research library. *Journal of the American Society for Information Science,* 30, 1979, 88-92.

Wessel, C.J. Criteria for evaluating technical library effectiveness. *ASLIB Proceedings,* 20, 1968, 455-481.

White, G.T. Quantitative measures of library effectiveness. *Journal of Academic Librarianship,* 3, 1977, 128-136.

Whitlatch, J.B. and Kieffer, K. Service at San Jose State University: survey of document availability. *Journal of Academic Librarianship,* 4, 1978, 196-199.

Wiberly, S.E., Jr. Journal rankings from citation studies: a comparison of national and local data from social work. *Library Quarterly,* 52, 1982, 348-359.

Wiemers, E., Jr. *Materials Availability in Small Libraries: a Survey Handbook.* Urbana, University of Illinois, Graduate School of Library and Information Science, 1981. Occasional Papers No. 149.

Williams, G.E. et al. *Library Cost Models: Owning Versus Borrowing Serial Publications.* Chicago, Center for Research Libraries, 1968.

Williams, R. Weeding an academic lending library using the Slote method. *British Journal of Academic Librarianship,* 1, 1986, 147-159.

Wills, G. and Christopher, M. Cost/benefit analysis of company information needs. *Unesco Bulletin for Libraries*, 24, 1970, 9-22.

Wood, F. *Evaluation of a University Library's Catalogue*. Canberra, Australian National University, 1984.

Wood, J.B. et al. Measurement of service at a public library. *Public Library Quarterly*, 2, 2, 1980, 49-57.

Zipf, G.K. *Psycho-Biology of Language*. Boston, Houghton Mifflin, 1935.

Zweizig, D. and Rodger, E.J. *Output Measures for Public Libraries*. Chicago, American Library Association, 1982.

Index

Abstracting service evaluation, 31
Academic excellence related to size of collection, 20
Access versus ownership, 11, 139
Accessibility factors affecting reference service, 120
Accessibility factors in use of information sources, 10, 28
Accessibility of information services, 10
ACRL standards, 19
Adaptability to changing conditions, 11-12
Additional copies, 100-102
Aging of publications, 72-75
Aguilar, W., 42, 49, 168
Ahl, R.E., 80, 182
Alexander, A.J., 33, 145, 179
Allen, T.J., 10, 28, 168
Allocation of resources, 6, 142-143
Altman, E., 92, 168
American Library Association, 82, 168
Association of College and Research Libraries, 19
Automated circulation systems in collection evaluation, 35-36, 40
Availability factors, 13-15, 100-102
Availability of materials, 9, 90-103
Availability on the shelf, 90-103

Baker, S.L., 80, 168
Ballard, T., 150-168
Bastille, J.D., 79, 177
Baughman, J.C., 64, 168
Baumol, W.J., 20, 168
Beilby, A., 50, 172
Bell, G.H., 50, 181
Benchmark studies, 6-7
Benefits of library service, 5-6, 154-162
Benham, F., 112-113, 150, 168, 181
Bennion, B.C., 64-65, 168
Berdie, D.R., 165, 168

Berry, R., 112, 175
Betts, D.A., 18, 168
Bibliographic checking in collection evaluation, 21-32
Bibliographies suitable for collection evaluation, 22
Birbeck, V.P., 113, 169
Bland, R.N., 23, 169
Blau, P.M., 20, 169
Bobick, J.E., 28, 66, 177
Bommer, M.R.W., 52, 92, 169
Bonn, G.S., 42, 169
Books Are For Use, 8
Books per capita, 17-18
Borkowski, C., 52, 169
Bourne, C.P., 6, 30-31, 151, 169
Bradford distribution, 34, 146-149
Bradford, S.C., 34, 146, 169
Braunstein, Y.M., 5, 169
Broadus, R.N., 65, 169
Brookes, B.C., 77, 169
Brophy, P., 166, 169
Broude, J., 68-69, 169
Buckland, M.K., 32, 41, 52, 76, 100-101, 169-170, 174
Bunge, C.A., 112, 121, 170
Burns, R. W., Jr., 166, 170
Burr, R.L., 19, 21, 29, 170
Burton, R.E., 72, 170
Buzzard, M.L., 28, 170
Byrd, G.D., 48, 170

Cain, A.M., 112, 180
Capability index, 95-96
Carlson, G., 111, 170
Catalog use studies, 82-89, 104-105, 135-136
Changing needs of users, 11-12
Checkout samples, 34-35
Chelton, M.K., 166, 170